AUBURN

A California mining camp comes of age

Other books distributed by Gilmar Enterprises:
Unspoken Thoughts
by Richard Latter Gilberg
Pumpkin Cookbook
compiled by R.L. Gilberg
illustrations by M. Gilberg

AUBURN

A California mining camp comes of age

M.E. Gilberg

Mary E. Gilberg

GILMAR PRESS
Newcastle, California

FIRST EDITION

Copyright © 1986 By Gilmar Press

All rights are reserved, including the right to reproduce this book or portions in any form.

Library of Congress Catalog Card Number 86-081117

ISBN: 0-936402-04-0

A GILMAR PRESS PUBLICATION
Designed And Distributed By:
GILMAR ENTERPRISES
P.O. Box 597
Newcastle, California 95658
U.S.A.

DEDICATION

To Dick who helped me get started and to Lu who helped me finish.

PREFACE

This book grew out of my curiosity about the community I first explored and later moved to in 1970. As time permitted during the intervening years I found myself researching bits and pieces of information about Auburn and its environs. Frequently I found myself sidetracked pursuing paths that took me into many intriguing corners of Auburn's history. These were new to me and may also be new to the reader.

Finding myself with a sizable collection of information, I decided to put it into book form and to share it with anyone who may be inquisitive about Auburn. This book is not the complete definitive history of Auburn. It does represent the product of my research efforts in satisfying my inquisitiveness.

For information presented as fact, I have made every effort to identify authoritative source documents. Those readers whose interest in Auburn may be stimulated by this book and who may wish to pursue areas of special interest, will find included notes, bibliography and research resources.

Part of the fun of this project was in locating photographs, maps and other documents. They helped me picture not only the city but the time I was exploring. I have included many of them in this book. A credit list is at the end of this book.

This book is a journey, with occasional detours, through the growth and development of Auburn, California. I hope it adds as much to your appreciation of this interesting foothill town as the researching and writing of it has added to mine. Please, enjoy the trip.

M. E. Gilberg
August, 1986

ACKNOWLEDGEMENTS

I am most appreciative of the help I received in the researching and writing of this book.

Arline Lutton, Librarian, Auburn Journal, was helpful in my early research. The Auburn Chamber of Commerce provided me with useful preliminary information. As my research progressed, the staff of both the Placer County Museum and the Auburn-Placer County Library were most cooperative. I am grateful to the help I received from Bruce Becker, Placer County Office of Education, as I researched school history. I especially appreciate the help I received from Sandra J. Elder, State Historical Resources Commission. She provided me with information, loaned photographs and gave me access to their library. It was here I got many useful leads in my search for specifics about Auburn.

The staffs of The Bancroft Library and The Huntington were helpful in providing me with information and photographs. The staffs of the California State Library and the California State Archives were cooperative, as always. I am particularly grateful to Ellen Schwartz, California State Railroad Museum Library, for her information and photographs. The library staff at American River College allowed me to photograph the "Acorn" press and Mr. and Mrs. Delmar provided me with much needed information about Auburn's first printing press. They also shared additional information about the Honorable J. A. Filcher. The staffs of the Placer County Clerk's Office, the Placer County Recorder's Office, the Auburn District Cemetary, and the Information Officer at Folsom Prison all deserve acknowledgement for their assistance.

I am particularly grateful to Mel Locher, Amy Rasmussen, Pete Hawkins and Sister Mary Elizabeth for taking time from their busy schedules to talk with me. Lee Photography was most helpful in locating and identifying photographs. George Bukowski was invaluable in helping with the final editing.

My very special thanks to Dick Gilberg for his help and encouragement throughout this entire project.

CONTENTS

1. **Explorers, Colonists and Gold** 1
   - The Explorers 1
   - The Colonists 2
   - The Gold 5
   - Through The Isthmus of Panama 7
   - Women Through The Isthmus 10
   - The Miners 11

2. **The Mining Camp Becomes A Town** 17
   - Auburn At The Crossroads 17
   - The Indians 19
   - Auburn's First Printing Press 20
   - Fires 22
   - The Blacks 23
   - The Lynching 25
   - Churches 28
   - Schools 30
   - Health Care 33
   - The Letter 35

3. **Auburn In The 1860s** 37
   - Struggle For Law And Order 37
   - Stagecoaches 38
   - The Pony Express 41
   - The Railroad 42
   - The Chinese 43
   - The Trip East 48
   - Remembrances 50
   - The Crandalls 53
   - Time Of Prosperity And Change 53

4. **Auburn In The 1870s** 61
   - Time Of Discontent 61
   - Auburn Continues To Grow 62
   - Changes In Mining 63
   - Auburn Considers Alternative Industries 63
   - Auburn Moves Into The 1880s 67
   - Local Indians 68
   - Auburn Recruits "home seekers" 69
   - The Japanese 72

xi

5.	**Auburn Moves Into The 20th Century**		**77**
	Culture Moves East	77	
	The "New" Court House	81	
	Labor Unrest	82	
	Toward The Twentieth Century	83	
	An Auburn Tragedy	84	
	Another Auburn Fire	86	
	Auburn Moves Into The Twentieth Century	86	
6.	**Auburn Comes Of Age**		**95**
	Automobiles And Aeroplanes	95	
	Women In Auburn	99	
	Health/Social Problems	99	
	World War I	100	
	The Great Depression	102	
	World War II	108	
	The DeWitt Army General Hospital	109	
	The Road Back	112	
7.	**Auburn — The Next Fifty Years**		**115**
	The Price Of Progress	115	
	How To Use DeWitt Army General Hospital	115	
	Auburn In The 1950s And 1960s	116	
	End Of An Era	118	
	The Future	119	
	Auburn — 1986	120	

Epilogue   121

Notes   123

Bibliography   133

Illustration Credits   139

Colophon   141

ILLUSTRATIONS

Auburn, California (map)..facing page	1
Listing from Directory, 1861...	3
Trading In The Mines..	6
Route through the Isthmus of Panama (map)...................................	7
Crossing The Isthmus..	8
Mrs. H. J. Crandall...	10
Life At The Diggins — Supper Time..	12
View of Auburn, California — Placer County, 1851...........................	14
Auburn appears for the first time on a map, 1851.............................	15
Map of the Gold Region, 1851...	16
Auburn, built on the slopes of Rich Ravine, 1857.............................	18
Auburn's First Printing Press..	21
The Placer Herald (advertisement)..	22
Old Town Firehouse..	23
Black Miner at Auburn Ravine, 1852..	24
Petition From Placer County, 1858...	27
The Methodist Church — Then and Now...	28
St. Theresa's Church...	29
The Sierra Normal College..	32
Placer County Hospital — prior to 1920..	34
County Map, California, 1860..	36
In Memory of Geo. M. Martin..	37
The California Stage Company (article and advertisement)................	39
Concord Stage (at the rear of the Freeman Hotel).............................	40
Old Chinese Houses built in fifties	44
Chinese Laundries, Old Town..	45
Railroad and Stage Lines, 1909...	47
Auburn Depot after 1865..	48
List of Pioneers — Excursion Trip of 1869.......................................	49
Recorded when Depot burned (1870)...	51
West's Hotel on Borland Ave., 1869...	52
Crandall Avenue (map)..	54
Auburn Businesses Advertise (advertisements)..........................	56 & 57
Map of California (Gray's Atlas) 1873..	58
Freeman Hotel, Auburn — circa 1900..	59
California Sacramento Sheet 1887-88 (map).....................................	60
American Hotel, 1900 (advertisement)...	63
Map of Bernhard Subdivision, 1895..	64
Bernhard Winery, (Placer Arts League Gallery One)...........................	65
Memorial Day Parade..	66
Old Auburn Post Office...	69
"Old Business Section of Lower Auburn"...	70
Auburn Fire House at the "head of Railroad Street"...........................	71

xiii

Lower Auburn – circa 1900	73
Snow In Auburn	74
Placer County, 1892 (map)	75
Auburn at the turn of the Century (map)	76
Central Square and the Auburn Opera House – pre-1900	78
Auburn Opera House, 1946	79
Placer County Court House (with bell)	80
New County Court House, 1894	81
Map of Southern Pacific Company Lines, 1902	82
Adolph "Dolphy" Weber, 1905	85
Placer County Bank construction, 1912-1913	86
Freemann Tract, 1891 (map)	87
Freeman Hotel at Railroad Avenue	87
Train wreck near the Cherry Street Bridge	89
The Overland Limited and a Local collide at Auburn	90
Train comes through Lower Auburn, 1909	91
Fourth of July Parade	92
The Placer Herald Building	93
The Placer Herald "sign"	93
Lincoln Way, Auburn (before 1911)	94
Lincoln Way, Auburn (after 1911)	94
City Bus – 1910	96
Cars in Lower Auburn	96
Old Car on Lincoln Way – 1913	97
"Bus" outside the Auburn Hotel, 1914	97
Women at work in Auburn – circa 1910	98
Placer County Republican – circa 1907	99
Armistice Celebration in Central Square, November 11, 1918	101
WPA "wall" at Forest Hill Avenue	104
Lincoln Way with Old Auburn Post Office	105
Lincoln Way, 1920	105
Lincoln Way, late 1930s	106
Lincoln Way, 1941	106
Lincoln Way (looking East) – 1930s or 1940s	107
Lincoln Way at the Freeman Hotel – 1941	107
DeWitt Army General Hospital	109
"Why?"	111
The Court House – Then (before 1913) and Now (1986)	113
Lower Auburn – circa 1900	114
Old Well At The Plaza	116
Lincoln Way – 1950s	117
Orleans Hotel, Auburn	119
Change	121
Upper California, 1850 (map)	122

AUBURN A California mining camp comes of age

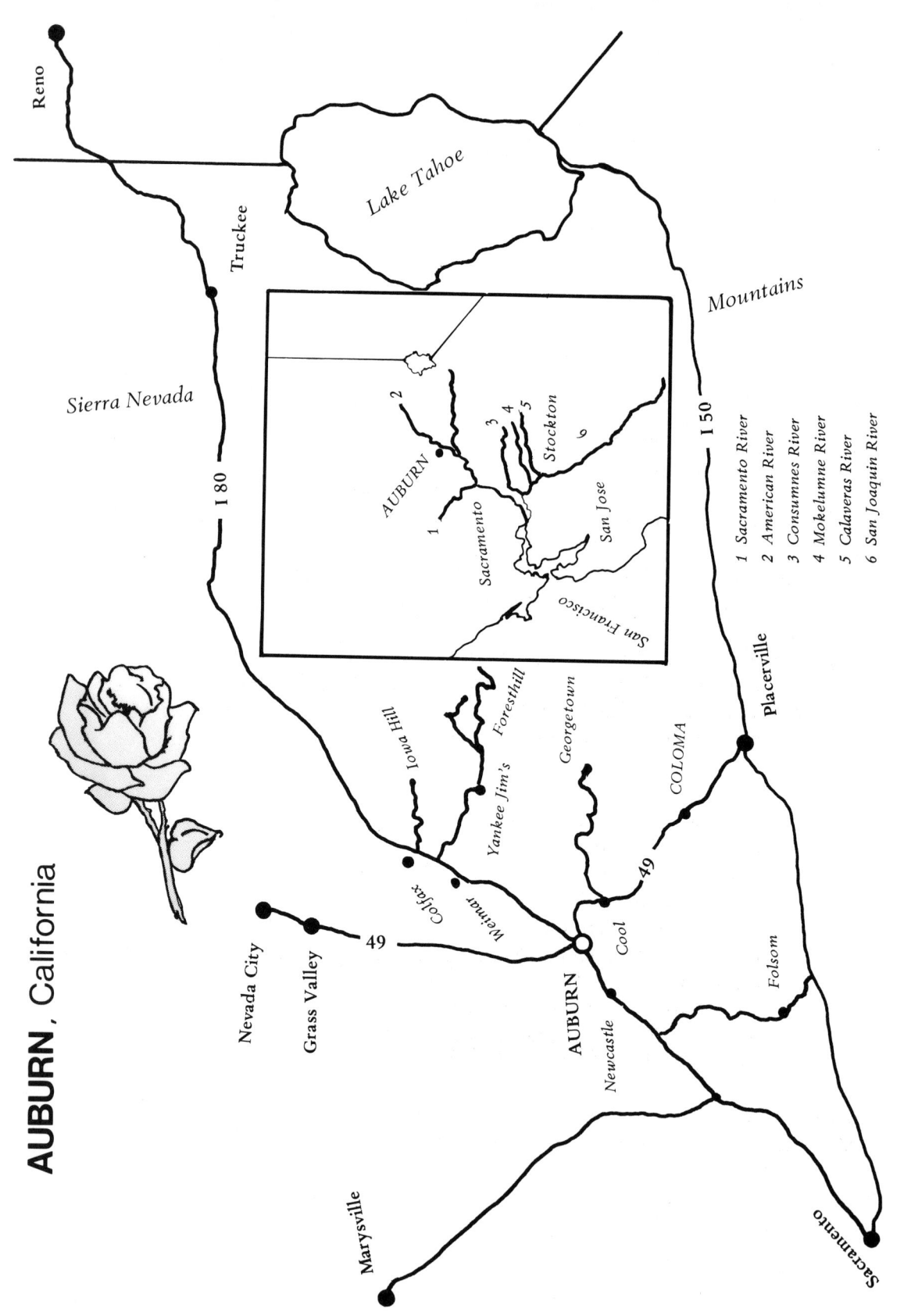

1

Explorers, Colonists And Gold

The Explorers

Gold helped to create Auburn, California, but its unique location at the crossroads of surrounding communities allowed it to survive and grow.

Westward migration had already started when that historic discovery was made at Sutter's sawmill in early 1848. The gold rush that followed hastened the movement toward California and directed attention to the foothills. However, those early gold seekers were not the first to come to what is now the Auburn area. History tells us that Indians have lived here for generations but Spaniards also traveled these foothills.

Gabriel Moraga was an Ensign in the San Francisco Company, a military force under Spanish rule, charged with protecting the California missions. He left San Jose Mission on September 25, 1808, with a company of eleven men. Their task was to find a suitable site for a new mission; one with sufficient numbers of unconverted Indians.

> "He forded the San Joaquin River, just a little below its junction with the Calaveras River, close by the site of the present city of Stockton. He then ascended the Calaveras River its entire length, without discovering a suitable location for a prospective Indian Mission. From here he proceeded northward to the Mokelumne River and, according to the diary, ascended this river also with the same result. He next tried his luck on the Consumnes River, then struck northward to the American River, crossing the latter a little below the present town of Auburn."[1]

This exploration took Moraga and his company further into the Sierra Nevada Mountains than any white men had gone before.[2] On October 7, 1808,

> "...we broke camp...and continued in the same direction to the river discovered yesterday, to which we gave the name Las Llagas."[3]

It must have been with disappointment that Ensign Gabriel Moraga and his men returned to the mission at San Jose. Their twenty-nine day trip ended without finding a new mission site in this area. Moraga did locate and name a river, Las Llagas. In the Spanish of his day this probably meant cut or deep wound. The Spanish speaking Indians of the area would later call this river, Rio de Los Americanos. We know it today as the American River.

There is no indication that Moraga returned to the Auburn area. The Indians continued to live here as they had for years. Over the next two decades, from 1810 to 1830, it is possible that mountain men ventured into the Auburn area. Such men lived off the mountains' natural resources and were known to have trapped for furs on the San Joaquin and Sacramento rivers in the early 1800s.[4] California's isolation gradually eroded as men such as these penetrated further into the mountains.

Two years before Ensign Gabriel Moraga found and identified the American River, another event was taking place that would affect California history. The Lewis & Clark Expedition, sponsored by the United States government, began its three year journey to the Pacific Coast and back by traveling down the Ohio River in August of 1803.[5]

Journeying with the Lewis & Clark Expedition was a Shoshone woman by the name of Sacajawea. She was born about 1784 and captured as a child by the Minnetarres tribe. Later her captors gambled her away to a Frenchman named Toussaint Charboneau. She became his wife and they were living in the Dakotas when Lewis & Clark reached there. Sacajawea and Charboneau were engaged as guides to the expedition. While wintering at Fort Mandan, Jean Baptiste Charboneau was born to Sacajawea on February 11, 1805. Sacajawea, while carrying her infant son on her back, proved to be a resourceful and courageous guide.

Jean Baptiste Charboneau received his education in America and Europe. He traveled extensively, as a young adult, in Europe and Africa. Some say he was the friend and traveling companion of Prince Wilhelm of Germany who introduced Charboneau at court in the 1820s. Charboneau engaged in adventurous activities during his lifetime. One of these was serving as a guide for the Mormon Battalion.

The Colonists

In 1846 the United States declared war on Mexico. On July 16th of that year the Mormon Battalion formed at Council Bluffs, Iowa Territory. These Mormons were immigrants in search of a home. They were encouraged to volunteer for service in California by President Polk as part of his plan for American expansion. Once the Mormons in this battalion had completed their year of service in the Mexican conflict, they planned to settle in California. The Mormons survived their difficult overland journey with the help of such guides as Charboneau. He is remembered in a firsthand account as being "brave" and a man with great "presence of mind."[6] Once discharged in California, some Mormons stayed and helped build a sawmill in the area later called Coloma, California. They were destined to participate in a discovery that would change the course of events in California forever.

Other Mormons were heard of in these California foothills after the disbanding of the battalion. The following recollection by William P. Bennett is of a Mormon family and the birth of their child. This may have been the first white child born in this area.

> "On the 25th day of December, 1849, on Canyon Creek, two miles from Georgetown, Placer County, California, the wife of William George Wilson gave birth to a twelve pound boy baby. This was the first child born in camp...The baby brought luck with it, for on the day it was born, Wilson made a big find in his claim. He struck a crevice that was piled full of course gold. He took out $3,000 in one pan. It was all in nuggets, the largest of which was worth over $300...Bill Wilson was a Mormon and later returned to Salt Lake City."[7]

Jean Baptiste Charboneau also tried his hand at mining in California. In late 1848 a J. B. Charboneau reportedly joined a mining camp at Buckner's Bar, east of what was to become Auburn.[8] Although verification is meager, he is probably the John B. Charbonnean listed in a local directory of 1861 as clerk at the Orleans Hotel in Auburn.[9] For the son of Sacajawea, who rode on his mother's back across much of this country, companion to royalty, mountain man, miner, hotel clerk and sometimes guide, life ended during one more adventure. Charboneau is remembered on a historical monument at Danner, Oregon,

"...he left California Gold Fields for a new strike in Montana, contracted pneumonia en route, reached Inskip's Ranch and here died on May 16, 1866."

These are a few of the people

```
Crandall J. R. Sec'y Bear River Co.  Court st.                          Auburn
Conway James, tailor,                bds. Orleans Hotel,                do
Crawford & Openshaw, Temple Saloon, cor. Com. & Court sts.              do
Credit J. G.                         bds. Soda Factory, East st.        do
Caust Jacob, carpenter,              Sacramento st.                     do
Crutcher W. M. Deputy Sheriff,       Court House,                       do
Curtis, E. J. teamster,              Geo. Willment's store,             do
Conner John, District Collector,     bds. American Hotel,               do
Clancy John, laborer,                bds. Orleans Hotel,                do
Charbonnean John B. clerk,           Orleans Hotel,                     do
Coulter Day, miner,                  Ill. and Sac. roads,               do
Cross Thos. tinner,                  Sacramento st.                     do
Clark Jas. H. prop. Yankee Jim's S.L.                                   do
Christopher B. miner,                Millertown
Collins James, farmer,               Spanish Flat
Castello James, miner,               N. Ravine, Millertown,
Crus A. miner,                       Schnable's Quartz Mills, Ophir
Cunningham M. miner,                                                    do
Choate D. merch't and Dist. Collector, Main st.                         do
Choate M. clerk,                     Main st.                           do
Choate N. miner,                     Main st.                           do
Cory Isaac, blacksmith,              Main st.                           do
Curtis D. B. miner,                  North Ravine,
Cummings H. farmer,                  Ophir
Curtis George, farmer,               do
Culleun Geo. prop. El Dorado Saloon, Main st. Gold Hill
Campbell Wm. blacksmith,             do    do    do
Crocker & Young. merchants,          do    do    do
Crocker C. E. of firm C. & Y.        do    do    do
Clary S. meat pedler,                Ham & Harford, Gold Hill
Challioll Geo. miner,                Gold Hill
Coleman Thos. W. miner,              Virginia
Colburn Thos. miner,                 do
Cowen J. B. miner,                   do
Carter J. farmer,                    Auburn Ravine
Cadellon W. farmer,                  Danesville
Crosby —. farmer,                    do
Conneyham John, miner,               Fox's Flat
Cook J. D. B. farmer,                Lincoln
Conner Patrick, laborer,             Applegate's Ranch, Lisbon
Curtis Hiram, laborer,               do    do    do
Craig John, clerk,                   Main st Illinoistown
Ciouse Jas. blacksmith,              Illinoistown
```

Courtesy Placer County Museum

Directory of The County of Placer, 1861

3

whose personal fortunes shaped the history of California which ultimately led to the Auburn we know today.

The Lewis & Clark Expedition was thus instrumental in ending California's isolation from the eastern United States. By 1841 John Bidwell led the first large group of forty-eight wagons to California over the Oregon Trail. Americans continued moving west. Border disputes erupted between the young country developing new borders and other nations with interests in the west. A dispute arose with England over the Oregon-Canadian boundary. Then with Mexico, which resulted in war and ended in the Treaty of Guadalupe Hidalgo in 1848.

President Polk was determined to secure California for the Americans. To this end he encouraged the formation of the Mormon Battalion. He also directed Colonel Jonathan Drake Stevenson to recruit young men, skilled in the trades of the times. First, to claim California from Mexico and then to remain as colonists in the newly acquired American territory. He established recruiting offices in several New York locations. Once the companies were formed, they marched off to Governor's Island in New York harbor for military training. One such young man, Edward, from Bath, Steuben County, New York, joined Company J of the New York Volunteers on June 26, 1846. He left Bath with other,

> "...intelligent and vigorous young men of many different trades, excellent habits, urbane manners and enterprising spirits...amid the acclamations of the mass of people assembled at the wharf."[10]

Other authors have described these recruits in less flattering terms.

> "In 1846 Colonel Jonathan Drake Stevenson headed west around the Horn with a scapegrace rabble recruited from New York's political wards, oyster cellars and gin mills..."[11]

Around Cape Horn they came. The young man from Bath, New York, was aboard the "Susan Drew", and arrived at Yerba Buena (San Francisco) on March 7, 1847. He traveled on to Monterey, and finally moved on to the Regiment's Headquarters at Los Angeles where he received his discharge on September 18, 1848.[12]

After their disbandment, the New York Volunteers scattered throughout California. Some made their way back home, and others became famous names in California's history. Some came to mining camps near Auburn Ravine and may have helped name Auburn. Young Edward, so far from his New York home, made his way to Placer County in 1848. He introduced the Angora Goat to this area. He became a Democratic delegate to a California State Convention and served as a Captain in the California Volunteers during the Civil War. By the early 1880s, Edward D. Shirland was an Auburn resident and stockraiser with 1200 acres of land.[13]

Even with all of these events, by the winter of 1847-1848, California's future seemed limited. Trade and most exploration had been along the coast. The gold discovery in 1842 by a Mexican rancher in southern California had been of no lasting consequence. Americans and English had seen possible economic gain in cattle raising and by taking advantage of Mexico's neglectful rule, were attempting expansion. There had been traders, trappers and whalers and some settlers had made it over the Oregon Trail. In 1846 the Donner Party had tried another route to California with disastrous results. President Polk's plans for California had seen the Mormon Battalian travel overland and the New York Volunteers come around Cape Horn. The colonizing of California was moving slowly. This part of California would have become just a nondescript addition to the United States had it not been for the discovery in 1848.

The Gold

James Wilson Marshall had agreed to build a sawmill for John A. Sutter on the South Fork of the American River about forty miles from Sacramento. The mill neared completion. Early one morning in mid-January, 1848, Marshall went to inspect the tailrace (a channel conducting refuse away in the water) of the mill. The glittering gold ore he found there changed the course of California's history.

Shortly after Marshall's discovery California was formally ceded on February 2, 1848, by Mexico to the United States. This gold find brought little attention outside of the local area until Spring. By April and May of 1848, the newspapers were beginning to take the gold discovery seriously. Sam Brannon shouted, "Gold! Gold! Gold!," on the streets of San Francisco in May, 1848. The Chilean Brig, "J. R. S.," in San Francisco Bay made the first known gold buy on May 3, 1848. The gold rush was on![14]

The first to get to the gold at Coloma were those already there and those in Sacramento who saw an opportunity to strike it rich. The Mormons discharged from the Mormon Battalion had gone to work for Marshall, building the mill. They left Coloma in February or March of 1848 and located the second major gold find on a river bar. This area near Folsom, California, would later be called Mormon Island.

Indians, Mexicans and Chileans were also in the area of the gold discoveries. Research shows that natives of Chile left their hide and tallow trading ships in San Francisco when word of gold reached them.[15] Local tradition places Claude Chana at Auburn Ravine in May, 1848. Chana, a Frenchman, is said to have,

> "...first turned the precious metal to light in the Dry Diggings of Placer County on the 16th of May, 1848."[16]

He spent only a few weeks here before moving on to more lucrative diggings. Steele, in describing Auburn, writes the following concerning the discovery of gold in the Auburn area:

"The town of Auburn is one of the oldest in the State, having been a mining camp of considerable importance early in 1849. Of the first discovery of gold upon its site, or in its neighborhood, there is at this time no reliable account; but when the writer of this article passed the spot in the first days of July, 1849, the ravines which converged in what is now the Plaza showed signs of having been wrought to some extent during the previous rainy season. The only persons at work, however, at that time were two Chilenos panning in Rich Ravine, a short distance above where the American Hotel now stands and a white man with a rocker upon the Main Auburn Ravine, near the present bridge on the turnpike. About the middle of July, Wm. Gwynn and H. M. House started trading-posts here, and a considerable population began to accumulate. Up to this time the place had been known as Wood's Dry Diggings."[17]

There was a John S. Wood known to have mined in the Auburn Ravine area and in the 1920s a historian wrote,

"...some contend to this day that Wood first discovered gold in and near Auburn, in (as we now know it) Auburn Ravine."[18]

TRADING IN THE MINES

From John Frost's History of The State of California 1850

Fifty years before Lardner's work, the following was written in an 1875 Auburn City directory,

> "There is no authentic account of the first discovery of gold on its (Auburn) site but the work was probably done in the winter of 1848-1849."[19]

Word of Marshall's gold discovery reached the East too late for successful overland travel until the Spring of 1849. For many eager gold seekers, spring was too late and the six to eight months of travel around Cape Horn too slow. Those willing to brave the challenge and danger chose to travel through the Isthmus of Panama. The first travelers to make it safely through this route arrived in San Francisco aboard the "California" on February 28, 1849. History refers to them as the "First Forty-Niners."

Through The Isthmus Of Panama

In the early 1500s, explorers first crossed the Isthmus of Panama (a narrow strip of land, varying in width from 31 miles to 110 miles; bordered on both sides by water). Until the completion of the Panama Railroad in 1855 crossings were on foot, on mules, or on the backs of natives. By 1846 the United States had a treaty with New Granada (the name used by the early settlers from Granada, Spain, for the country now known as Columbia). This treaty guaranteed American citizens the right to travel across the Isthmus of Panama but didn't guarantee their safety. The hazards were many; strange climate and food, lost belongings, foreign language, swindlers, fever and injury or even death. Once across the Isthmus there was no assurance of a waiting ship. Crews abandoned their ships in San Francisco when they heard of the fortunes awaiting them in the gold fields. By the Spring and Summer of 1849, several thousand gold seekers were stranded in Panama. However, with American ingenuity, some of them demonstrated an enterprising spirit and even profited from the delay.

George K. Fitch, long time part-owner and editor of the San Francisco Bulletin, used this delay in Panama to start the short-lived Panama Star. He

Route through the Isthmus of Panama

CROSSING THE ISTHMUS

From John Frost's History of The State of California 1850

arranged with a local publisher to revive a failed Spanish weekly into a new English language newspaper, to supply materials and to print the paper. Fitch wrote the copy, set the type and handled sales to the several hundred Americans stranded with him. Five issues were produced with an extra on the day Fitch boarded the "Oregon," August 28, 1849, to finish his journey to the mines. Fitch arrived at Auburn with nine other men on October 18, 1849, and became disappointed with what he found. Later, he wrote to the readers of the Cleveland Herald that the,

> "...success of a few individuals is trumpeted abroad. The misfortunes of the many are kept in silence."[20]

Earlier, on March 12, 1849, James Delavan had boarded that same "Oregon" and later gave the following advice;

> "Yet, notwithstanding the many hardships and dangers of the Isthmus route, on the truth-loving pilgrim, I do assure you it is the best that can be travelled. That is, if any confidence can be placed on the narrations of those who have gone round Cape Horn, overland by Mexico, or across the Rocky Mountains. But be sure to secure a ticket for the steamers, and never trust a sail craft on the Pacific. And if possible, choose the dry season for the voyage. Be abstemious, long-suffering, and patient if you can for by much tribulation only, can aspirant for adventure reach the Golden Gates of California."[21]

The traveler through the Isthmus of Panama had to face two seasons, rainy and dry. The rainy season lasted from mid-April to mid-December with regular afternoon tropical showers. The rains made the narrow roads even more treacherous and disease in this climate was commonplace. Undaunted, the immigrants kept coming. By 1850 there was more information being published for the would be traveler to the gold fields of California.

> "Both steam and sailing vessels are constantly engaged in carrying freight and passengers from the principal ports of the Atlantic States to Chagres, the principal port on the eastern coast of the Isthmus. Tickets which will carry passengers to Chagres, and, after crossing the Isthmus, from Panama to San Francisco, can be purchased in New York, from whence to Chagres, the passage generally occupies about eight days, and has been accomplished in seven. The harbor in Chagres is a small but good one, for vessels of less than two hundred tons burden. It is protected by hills on all sides and towards the ocean, by a beetling cliff, jutting out into the sea, on the summit of which is the ancient and somewhat dilapidated castle of

The First White Woman, Who Ever Went to Auburn to Live.

Mrs. Crandall enjoys the distinction of having been the first white woman to arrive in Auburn in pioneer days, says the Placer Republican, and her memory contains everything that is of interest concerning the growth and history of this town and of the county. She has been closely identified with the material prosperity and with the social side of Auburn, and her pleasant residence at the junction of Railroad and High streets, is one of the finest here. Mrs. Crandall is a prominent member of the M. E. Church, a leader in charitable work, and she has been a liberal promoter of everything that was for public improvement. She is a favorite with old and young, and an honored and respected member of the community.

Mrs. H. J. Crandall.

Courtesy California State Library

This article appeared in **The Morning Call,** San Francisco, Tuesday, June 16, 1891.

The occasion was the celebration of Mrs. Harriet J. Crandall's seventy-eighth birthday.

The drawing is a facsimile of that which appeared in the article.

San Lorenzo. At the base of this cliff is the channel which forms an entrance to the town. Ignorance of this fact caused the wreck of several of the vessels which went from the United States to Chagres soon after the receipt of the news of the gold discovery."[22]

Women Through The Isthmus

Hundreds of Americans came through the Isthmus of Panama in those first few years. Most were young men seeking their fortune in the gold fields of California. However, some of these brave travelers were women. Mrs. Harriet J. Crandall of Illinois was one such woman having come through the Isthmus during the rainy season to join her husband. J. R. Crandall had come overland to California. He was already in the Auburn area developing the Bear River Ditch Company, which would later supply water to Auburn. When his wife joined him in December, 1851, she became the first white woman to come and stay in Auburn.[23]

There were other women who traveled this route. On November 13, 1854, a group, including eight nuns, left New York on the "Star of the West." In deference to their calling, they were able to travel the last twelve miles of the arduous Isthmus route in a wagon. Their first sight of the Pacific Ocean was a delight to them. They were less delighted with the sight of the half-naked natives who were to carry them to their steamer.

> "No wharves were provided for passengers en route to the North, and the custom was for the natives, somewhat scantily clad, to carry the passengers about fifty yards to a waiting skiff...the natives were prevailed upon to don pantaloons and shirts before carrying the reluctant sisters to the Pacific Steamer, 'Cortiz'."[24]

These eight women left the "Cortiz" on December 8, 1854. They were the first Sisters of Mercy to arrive in San Francisco. This Order would later establish Saint Joseph's Academy in Sacramento and the Motherhouse in Auburn.

The Miners

Three years before the arrival of the Sisters, Mrs. Crandall had made her way to Auburn and in the trip to the raw mining camp of the early 1850s had found that women were valued for a variety of services, but none more than their culinary skills.

> "We had some strange experiences coming up from Sacramento...when we had been about a day on the road we met a party of miners returning from the mines. They had been up there about a year, and when they saw me they nearly went crazy. You see they had not seen a white woman for so long, and they said that sometimes they had never expected to see one again. Nothing would satisfy them but we must camp right there and I should cook dinner for them. Of course I did it, and then they wanted me to take a share of their gold dust, but I wouldn't do that."[25]

Many miners, like the ones Mrs. Crandall met on the road from Sacramento, had not intended to stay long in the mining camps. They had planned to stay a few weeks, make their fortunes and return to their homes. The weeks turned into months and the diggings were not as rich as they had hoped or were led to believe. Many of these men were not prepared for that first winter and the "snow that fell in the mountains."[26]

The distance of history gives a romantic cast to those early days in the California mining camps. For the men and few women who lived through those harsh times, life was anything but romantic. Dr. Tyson wrote in 1849 what faced the early adventurer trying his luck in the search for California gold.

> "If I could convey to the reader an adequate conception of what a gold-seeker in California had to endure I would

LIFE AT THE DIGGINS—SUPPER TIME.

From John Frost's History of The State of California 1850

> scarcely be credited. Quarrying, the digging of canals, cellars, and wells, or all combined, are not capable of comparison with the intense hard labor, and almost unbearable privations he is compelled to undergo. None but a laboring man is fit for the business. He must have been inured to the most trying hardships from his earliest infancy, and have a constitution and frame of iron, to endure it for any length of time; sickness in some form often overtaking even the most robust, after a few weeks' toil. Many had been here since the preceding fall, and were no better off than on the day of their arrival. The majority leave with broken health and spirits, the consequence of exposure and privations to which they had been unaccustomed, and the utter prostration of their brilliant hopes."[27]

Some miners did strike it rich and returned to their homes or established themselves in California. Others found they were better able to make their fortunes providing goods and services to the mining community than by working the mines. Also, mining began to decrease in Auburn. As this occurred, the mining camp began to change. A miner in 1849 described Auburn quite different from a visitor ten years later.

> "About ten o'clock...August 2, 1849, we arrived at the diggings – North Fork Dry Diggings...now the site of Auburn, Placer County. There were only three or four tents there and perhaps a half dozen men...leaving the North Fork Dry Diggings (later sometimes called Woods). November, 1849, returned...to Auburn (then just given that name)."[28]

Following is a written account of Vischer when he visited Auburn in the spring of 1859;

> "We reached Auburn, located about twenty-three miles from Folsom at noon. Auburn has lost some of its mining activity. It has become the main refuge of the Chinese who make it their headquarters during their frequent expulsions from neighboring districts. Nevertheless, around noon when the stages coming from many directions meet here a very lively atmosphere is created. Most of this concentrates on main street around some American Hotels and a row of clothing stores."[29]

Many of California's early mining camps became ghost towns as the ore played out but Auburn was unique. Its location at the center of a network of roads to the surrounding mines allowed it not only to survive but to grow into a town of miners and merchants. As Auburn's population changed from the young transient adventurer seeking his fortune in gold to a stable community which included families, the unruly mining camp began to come of age.

Auburn is one of the oldest mining towns in the State. It is the seat of justice for Placer County, and is situated on the West Bank of the North Fork of American River, within three miles of the junction of the Middle and North Forks. The streets and town lots of this settlement have been considerably dug over for gold, and in many instances houses have been undermined for the same object. At present it is the principle trading point for the large number of miners congregated at Horse Shoe Bar, Smith's Bar, Oregon Bar, Dead Man's Bar, Murderer's Bar, and the less important mining localities for miles up and down the North Fork, as well as for a wide expanse of country on all sides, which abounds in dry diggings. Latterly considerable attention has been attracted to this place, in consequence of the discovery of numerous veins of goldbearing quartz; several crushing mills have recently been ordered for that neighborhood, and we learn that there are indications of immense wealth among the hills and river banks, many of which are nearly all white with the protruding quartz rock. Bear River, which at present empties into Feather River just above Nicolous, is soon to be turned from its original course by means of a canal thirty-five miles long, and when this great work is completed, which will be before many months, the entire volume of water will pass through Auburn, and disembogue in the American River. It will be creating a new River in California, and taking up one that already exists. This will have a most important effect on Auburn, as nearly all Placer County is highly auriferous, and when water becomes plenty, a large population will doubtless resort there to labor in the Placeres.

The above view was drawn and engraved by Mr. Thomas Armstrong, a most finished artist, whose numerous wood cuts of California towns and cities are justly celebrated.

View of Auburn, California - Placer County 1851 *Courtesy California State Library*

Auburn appears for the first time on a California map.
From B.F. Butler's Map of the Gold Region, California, 1851.

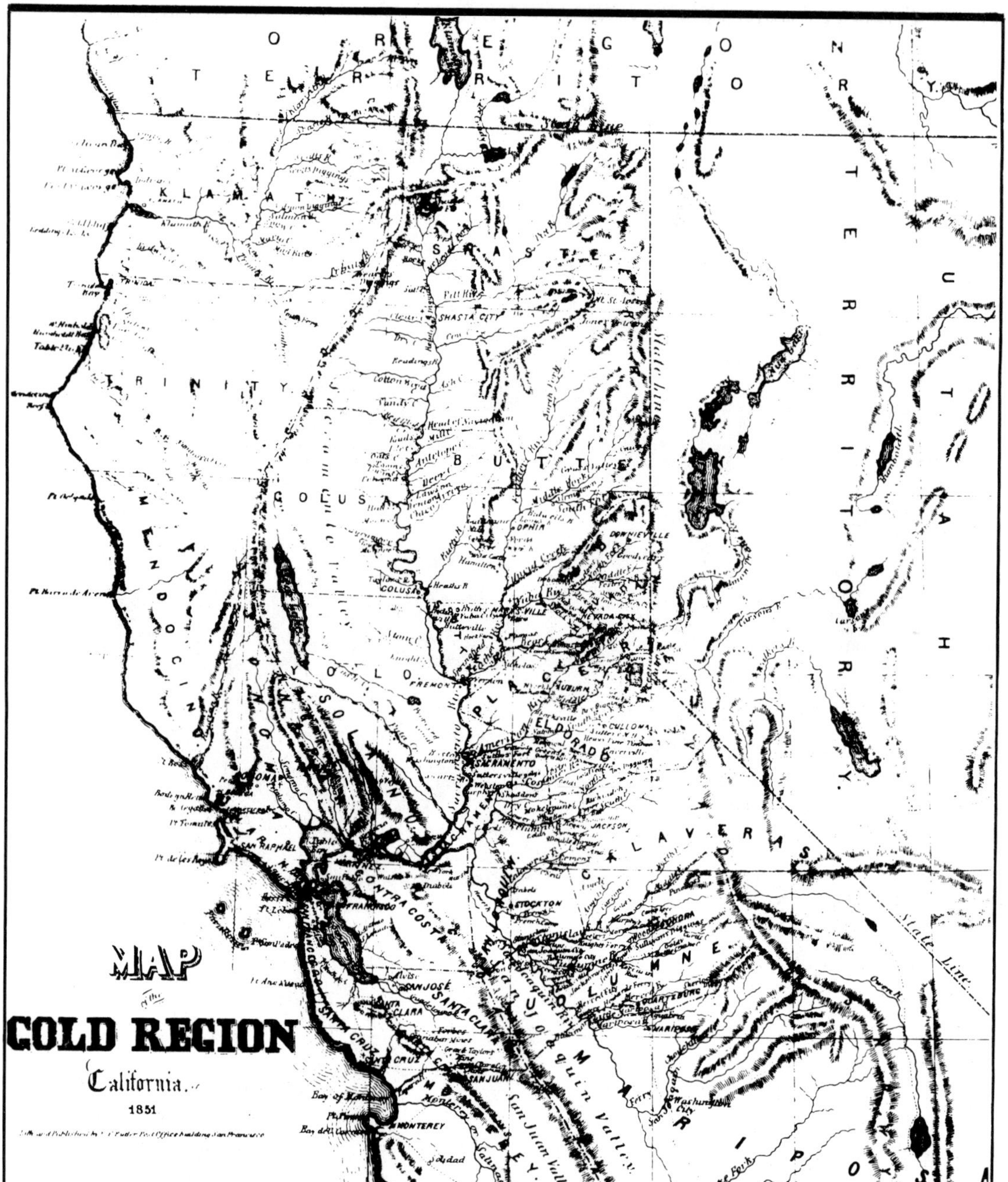

B. F. Butler's Map of 1851 issued from the Post Office Building, San Francisco.

2

The Mining Camp Becomes A Town

Auburn At The Crossroads

Marshall's discovery of gold at Sutter's Mill in January of 1848 began a monumental migration to California. Between 1848 and 1850 close to 50,000 new people came to try their luck in the Golden State. By 1850 they had put an estimated two million dollars into the American economy, contributing to the inflation of that year.[30]

When the gold rush began, some of those already in California abandoned their businesses and farms in favor of the gold fields. Those coming from other parts of the country, mostly young men willing to endure great hardships, left wives and families behind. In addition to the Panama and Cape Horn routes, they came overland, facing hostile Indians, starvation and cholera.

Americans were not the only ones lured by the call of California gold. The Placer County "Death Records Book 1873-1904" lists some of the countries these immigrants came from: Mexico, India, France, Portugal, Wales, England, Scotland, Ireland, Chili, Germany, China, Switzerland, Russia, New Zealand and Canada.

As the population grew more divergent, Americans became unwilling to share the diminishing gold. The result was repressive and exclusionary legislation such as the foreign miners tax and immigration restrictions. At times this competition with non-Americans erupted into violence.

> "...feeling against the Mexican miners and their kindred, culminated in the famous Foreign Miner's Tax Law of the first California legislature. The chief feature of this statute was a monthly tax of twenty dollars upon each foreigner engaged in mining. This was collected under a system of licenses, and forced many foreigners to abandon claims of their own to work for day wages...Agitation against the Chinese did not begin until 1851, since previous to that time they were not present in the mining camps in sufficient number to arouse prejudice...whole camps united to drive the Chinese out of their district. For example, two hundred Chinamen on the American River were expelled from their claims by sixty miners from Mormon Bar in the spring of 1852. The same sixty next

descended upon four hundred celestials who were hard at work farther down the river at Horse Shoe Bar."[31]

While mining was continuing in the area surrounding Auburn, the town itself began to change. Wm. Gwynn and H. M. House had established their trading-post in Auburn during the summer of 1849 and other merchants followed. The lure of gold drew men of different trades and professions. Some of these men found their fortunes by providing goods and services to the miners. It was an advantage to these businessmen to be at the hub of the surrounding communities. What was once a dusty mining camp at the edge of Auburn Ravine was to become an important trade and commerce center. Families began to arrive in Auburn in the early 1850s and the temporary cloth and board shacks of the transient mining camp were replaced with more substantial buildings. By the 1850s, Auburn had a school, hotels and stagecoach service. Postal service had begun as early as March of 1851. By June of 1852 the Methodist Episcopal Church had organized with fifteen members.

Courtesy California State Library

Auburn, built on slopes of Rich Ravine. From an old drawing made in 1857

Events were moving fast elsewhere in the state and country. The Mexican War ended. Shortly after the discovery of gold, California was ceded to the United States. In anticipation of statehood, California had its first Constitutional Convention at Monterey in October of 1849. By Fall of 1850 California had become the thirty-first state. Now from the East came the stirring of conflict between the states. But the citizens of Auburn were preoccupied with problems closer to them.

The Indians

The local Indians had not taken kindly to the white invasion. Although not as aggressive as the Plains Indians, some California Indians did engage in limited fighting with the settlers in this area. As the gold seekers crowded into California, they pushed aside the Indians. They disturbed and sometimes destroyed their way of life. Armed only with their primitive weapons and an occasional gun, the local Indians fought as long as they were able. Frost's History of the State of California, 1850, contains the following newspaper article:

> "About two weeks ago, a party of Indians came stealthily upon a few miners who were sleeping after their work was over in their tents on the North Fork, some twenty miles above Auburn. Before the Indians gave any warning to the whites of their presence, they killed two, wounded another, and then succeeded in making their escape. On Friday of last week, a trader, who was travelling with his team, was surrounded by Indians when about fifteen miles above Auburn. The arrows from their bows took effect upon his person, and he only saved his life by a precipitous flight. They carried off his coat which he left in his wagon, with $600 worth of gold dust in the pocket. They also robbed his wagon of several valuable articles. Upon receiving news of this attack at Auburn, a number of men set out on horseback, in pursuit of the Indians. They overtook them in a valley not far from Auburn, and found a large party of Indians drawn up to meet them. The Indians were armed with bows and arrows and had one gun. The whites attacked them, and soon put them to flight. The Indians left a considerable number of dead behind them; and it is supposed that they carried off many more. Two of the whites were wounded with the arrows of the Indians, but not fatally. It is believed by many of the miners that there are white men among the Indians, inciting them to hostilities. It is pretty certain that a German doctor has been leading them on their attacks. A meeting was held at Auburn, last Monday evening, to raise a company of volunteers for the purpose of scouring the country, and making war upon the Indians wherever found so long as they maintain a hostile position, and a number of men were enrolled."
>
> *Pacific News, May 15th, 1850*

The "whites" prevailed and the local Indians were overcome by superior weapons and greater numbers. Seven years later the local newspaper wrote in reference to the Indian Agents in Oroville, California, and their "corralling the Diggers,"

> "We hope the agents will next turn their attention this way and rid Auburn and its vicinity of a number of these creatures..."
>
> *The Placer Herald, September 12, 1857*

The written word was slow to reach the foothills in those early years but the people of Auburn were eager for news. By September 11, 1852, the first issue of The Placer Herald (Weekly Placer Herald) was published by Tabb Mitchell, Richard Rust and John McElroy.[32] Before that first month was over, they had printed a glowing account of Auburn which found its way one Monday morning, September 20, 1852, into the San Francisco Daily Alta California.

> "Placer County—The Placer Herald contains a long and interesting article concerning the principal town, resources, politics and prospects of that county. Auburn, the county seat, is situated on the Big or Auburn Ravine, and within about one mile of the North Fork of the American River, and four miles below the junction of the Middle and South Forks, and six miles South of the Bear River. It is a flourishing town, and was located in the early part of the summer of 1849. It is improving rapidly, and substantial buildings are daily erected. Three stages arrive and depart each day for Sacramento, one for Marysville, one for Grass Valley and Nevada, one for Yankee Jim's and one for Illinoistown. They are all doing a good business. The Bear River and Auburn Canal office is also there. The labor is now nearly completed of constructing a canal about fifty miles in length to conduct the waters of Bear River into the town of Auburn. The citizens there have taken a great amount of stock in the telegraph line, and a railroad from Sacramento to Nevada by way of Auburn, is in contemplation. The mines are considered to be as rich as any in the country."

The Placer Herald office burned in 1855. Rebuilt in 1858, it was torn down in the 1940s to make room for the expanding highway. Its first printing press survives to this day.

Auburn's First Printing Press

Auburn's first printing press is identified as an Adams press, manufactured by Seth Adams & Company, Boston, Massachusetts, in the 1840s. How it made its way to California is unclear. There has been speculation that it was the press Sam Brannon brought with him aboard the "Brooklyn" in 1846 and used to print the

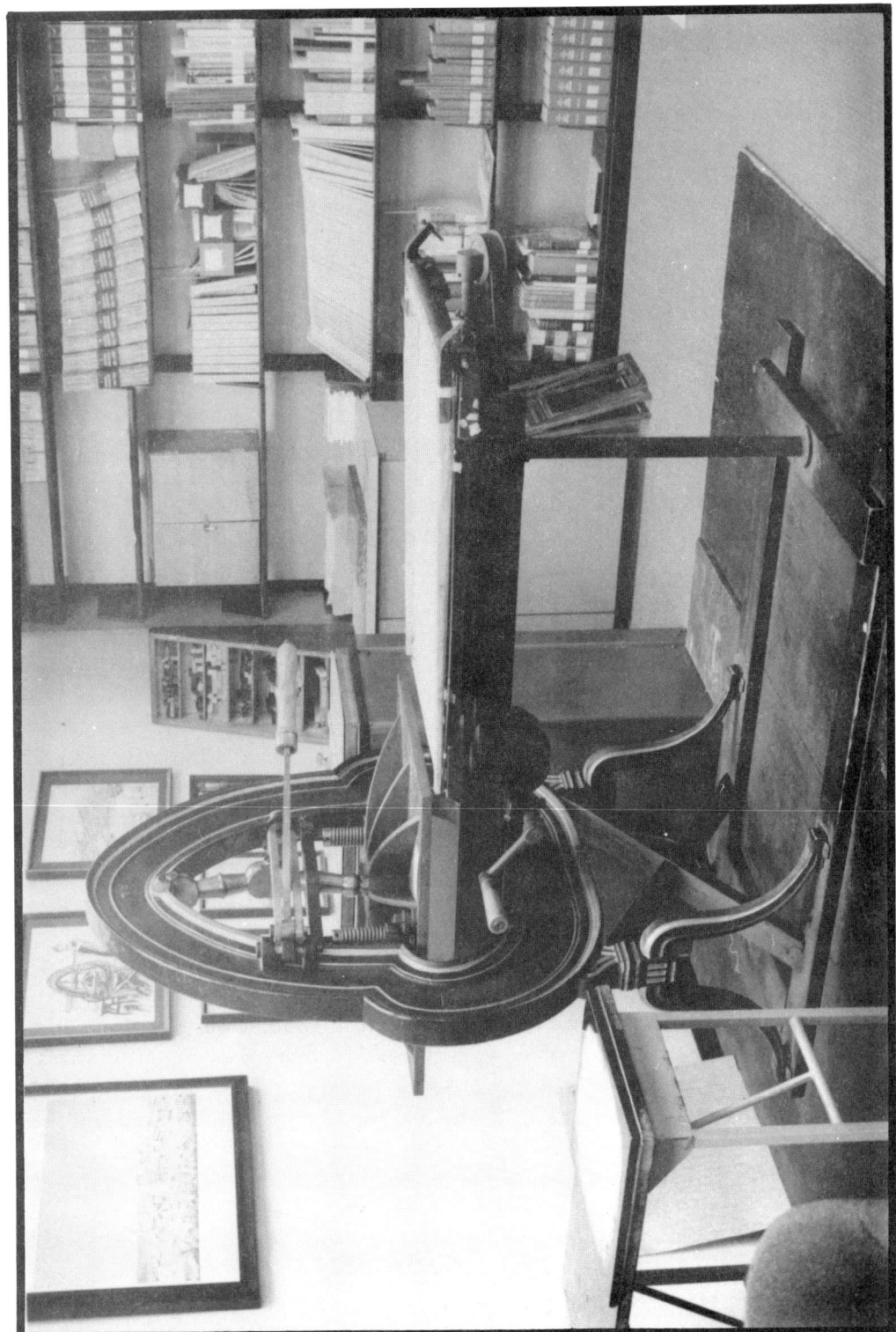

Auburn's First Printing Press

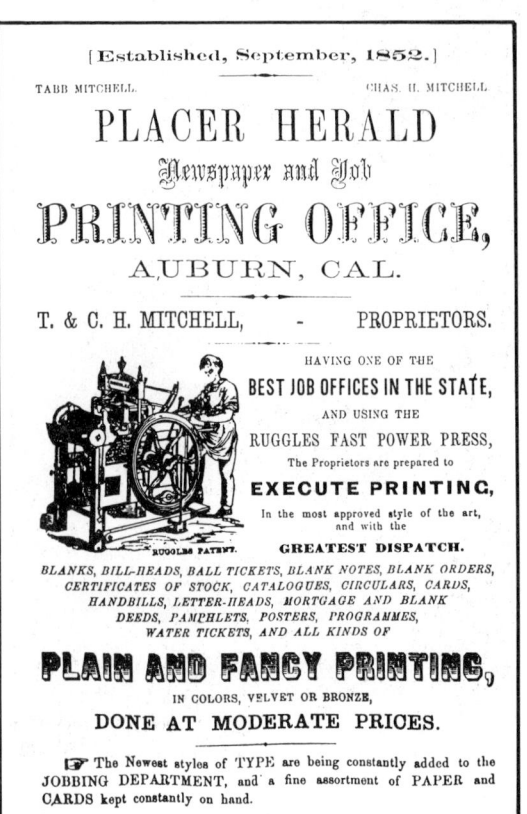

California Star, San Francisco's first newspaper. Even J. A. Filcher, owner of the Placer Herald from 1873 to 1900, writing to M. J. Ferguson, California State Librarian, on April 2, 1923, stated, "That it is the Brannon Press there is no doubt..." This has yet to be proven. What we do know is where this press has been these past one hundred and thirty four years.

The Placer Herald used the Adams "Acorn" Press to print the first Auburn newspaper in 1852. A cylinder press replaced the Adams in 1898 and Filcher sent the Adams Press "on tour." It spent the winter of 1898 at a mining fair in San Francisco — then loaned to the de Young Museum. In 1922 it was moved to the Days of '49 Celebration in Sacramento — then placed on display at the California State Library. By 1959 it was on its way back to Auburn, California. In 1963 the press again went "on the road." This time the press found a temporary home in the Columbia Gazette Building at Columbia State Park. By 1977 Auburn's first press returned to the "jurisdiction of the Filcher Family for restoration."

For those interested in seeing a well traveled Auburn pioneer, the Adam's "Acorn" Press can be seen as a restored working press in the California Room, third floor, American River College, Sacramento, California.[33]

Fires

Growing communities in California in the 1850s had many problems to overcome. Communications was one such problem for Auburn and fires were another. San Francisco had its fire of 1851 and Auburn its fire of 1855. The horse-drawn steam pumpers were in the process of being developed in Ohio in 1852. In November of that same year, Auburn's first volunteer fire fighters were organized to replace the old bucket brigade. It would be thirteen years later, in New York, before the country had its first paid fire fighters.

Paid or not, the volunteers and Auburn community rallied and fought in vain that afternoon of June 4, 1855, to save their town from a disastrous fire. The fire burned for over an hour and consumed eighty buildings. Auburn was devastated. Heroes come forth in disasters such as this and Auburn had a hero that day in Chesterfield Jackson.

Chesterfield Jackson was born in Kentucky in 1818 and married to Caroline Jackson (born in Missouri in 1828). By 1860 they had accumulated real property in the amount of $1800 and personal property amounting to $200. Quite an accomplishment for Black laundry workers in Auburn in the mid-1800s.[34] By 1865 Jackson found himself in court. He had sold his property on Union Street near the graveyard to James Howard. He disappeared into Nevada Territory leaving Jackson with a $379 note. With the help of his attorney, C. A. Tweed, Jackson prevailed in forcing a Sheriff's Sale on an early Saturday morning on April 8, 1865.[35]

Old Town Firehouse
Courtesy State Historical Resources Commission

On June 4, 1855, Chesterfield Jackson became a hero. Jackson was wounded early on by a "clumsy axeman."[36] This did not stop him. He continued to fight the fire and received accolades from his fellow citizens for the effort he put forth with "skill and judgment."[37] The Placer Herald reported five days after the fire,

> "...we would mention the faithful labors of a Negro man named Jackson, who assisted a great deal toward saving this public building."

The building he helped save was the Placer County Court House.

The Blacks

Blacks came to California at the time of the gold rush as freemen and with their owners from slave states. The first Black man with gold dust is known to have been in San Francisco in September of 1848.[38]

> "When the gold rush began in 1848, the black population in California was no more than a few dozen. They were a blend of the earlier, pre-American period, arrivals and those who

23

Black Miner At Auburn Ravine 1852

> came with the American conquerors of Mexican California... the California Negro population doubled in the first three years of the gold rush. By 1852 two thousand black men and women...were in the state."[39]

Although these numbers represent about 1% of the population of the time, many, like Chesterfield Jackson, contributed to California's history. That court house Jackson worked so hard to save in 1855 should have been the setting two and a half years later for another Black man.

The Lynching

Aaron Bracy's lifeless body hung limply from the tree on the outskirts of Auburn that February morning in 1858.

> "...Bracy was dragged...down East Street to an open field, opposite the present Veterans Memorial Hall, where he was lynched."[40]

Bracy was one of only a few Black men engaged in agriculture in the Auburn area. Reports differ whether Bracy sold land to Murphy or Murphy sold land to Bracy; however, on February 18, 1858, the two men argued about the land in question. The argument escalated. Bracy struck Murphy in the head with a steel pointed pickax and then walked into Auburn. Bracy surrendered to the Sheriff and was placed in jail. Local citizens went to Murphy's aid. He lived for a brief time after they reached him and told his version of the incident. Anger mounted in Auburn in the evening. By early the next morning, a mob stormed the jail and hung Aaron Bracy.

There was only one known attempt to stop this lawless act. Father John Quinn, pastor of Saint Rose's Catholic Church, Sacramento, regularly traveled to Folsom to conduct services. By 1858 he had extended his area of service to include Auburn. Pushed aside during the lynching he was unable to interrupt the mob action against Bracy. After hanging Bracy, the mob

> "...plundered the lynched man's home and burned it down. When Bracy's brother, Henry Bracy of Marysville, came to claim his brother's land, he found it occupied and he was driven away."[41]

The San Francisco newspapers reported Bracy's hanging as an "outrage." They suggested the Archy Lee decision had played a part in this Auburn tragedy.

Archy Lee came to California with his owner from Mississippi in the Fall of 1857. Once in California, Archy Lee attempted to secure his freedom. He was arrested. The lower court found Lee to be a free man. The California State Supreme Court, however, determined that while California was a free state, they would make an exception in this case. It was the first case of this kind in California and Lee's owner was an "inexperienced young man not in good health."[42] The decision, to return Archy Lee to slavery, took place in Sacramento on February 11, 1858. This was just eight days before Bracy was lynched in Auburn.

At the first Constitutional Convention in the Fall of 1849, before statehood, the following was adopted,

> "Neither slavery, nor involuntary servitude, unless for the punishment of crimes, shall ever be tolerated in this state."
> *Article I, Section 18*

However, California in the 1850s had on its books a,

> "...law which Disqualified Negroes and Mulattoes from being Competent Witnesses in the Courts of Justice in Cases or Proceedings, to which white persons are parties."
> *Section 14, passed April 16, 1850, amended, March 18, 1863.*

On Tuesday, February 2, 1858, in the California Assembly, Mr. Safford put forward a petition from Placer County. This petition requested repeal of the law disqualifying Negroes and Mulattoes as competent witnesses. This was seventeen days before the Auburn mob hung Bracy.

What part these events, the Dred Scott decision the year before and the pending Civil War had on the temper of Auburn after hearing that a black man had killed a white man is unknown. The violence against Blacks in Auburn was not over.

> "Outrage on Colored Men at Auburn — On Sunday night, 11th July, Auburn, says the Placer Herald, was disgraced by the acts of a crowd of men, who made an attack on three houses, occupied by colored men, and broke in the doors and windows, and destroyed most of the property in the buildings, amounting to several hundred dollars. There does not appear to have been the slightest provocation for the outrage — the sufferers being quiet and peaceable men. A general indignation has been expressed by the citizens in relation to the affair. The authorities will immediately take the matter in hand."
> *San Francisco Bulletin, July 12, 1858.*

Not everyone suffered the injustices wrought on Blacks in Auburn in 1858. A lawyer traveling through Auburn that same year had a very different and apparently positive experience.

To the Honorable Senate and Assembly of the State of California:

The undersigned, residents of the County of Placer, State of California, pray your Honorable Body to repeal so much of the Third paragraph of Section 394, of An Act entitled "An Act to Regulate Proceedings in Civil Cases in the Courts of Justice in this State, passed April 29, 1851, as relates to Negroes."

Also, to Repeal so much of Section 14, of An Act entitled "An Act Concerning Crimes and Punishments, passed April 16, 1850, as relates to Negroes and Mulattoes, viz: To Repeal those provisions of the law which Disqualifies Negroes and Mulattoes from being Competent Witnesses in the Courts of Justice in Cases or Proceedings, to which white persons are parties."

"*Compiled Laws of the State of California, Section* 394, *3d Paragraph*:"—Negroes, or Persons having one half or more negro blood, shall not be Witnesses in an action or proceeding to which a white person is a party.—*Page* 591.

Section 14:—No Black or Mulatto person shall be permitted to give evidence in favor of, or against, any white person: Every person who shall have one-eighth part, or more, of negro blood shall be deemed a Mulatto—*Page* 639.

SIGNATURES.	SIGNATURES.
D. W. Chipman	A Howard
Johanes Peterson	[illegible]
[illegible]	B. J. Breden
Horace Young	M. W. Emery
[illegible]	
[illegible]	Charles R. Clukey
John Blanchard	G. W. Allenberg
S. S. Willard	F. Miner
W. C. Barson	Richard Pollo[?]
Barney Tutt	J. F. Eneve
Ferdinand Haaffe	W. Lawrence
J. M. Miner	J. Hansen
J. B. Hamilton	J. Wheeling
John [illegible]	Thomas Gawrworth
J. W. D. Weed	Henry Webb
Obediah Ralston	Thos. D. Norcross
M. Seaman	Jacob Walker
John J. Burns	Z. Holms
George Tafft	P. Vidderman
John Whitney	H. Nety
J. W. Roberson	Augustine Labette
Oren Harman	R. Lee
J. S. Pratt	John McAlpin
William T. Johnson	William O'Neil
Geo. W. Stowel	A. F. Merrit

PETITION FROM PLACER COUNTY 1858 — *Courtesy California State Archives*

> "Took the stage for Auburn, to attend the case of Brady vs. Henn in the County Court of Placer Co...in the late afternoon, in the evening wen(t) with Hawkins up to the Court House and listened to the Auburn Brass Band and then came down to Davidson's and was entertained by the Cotillion Band...put up at the American. Tues. 16...in the evening went to the Chinese Theatre with Hawkins and saw them play."[43]

While the citizens of Auburn coped with Indian hostilities, lawlessness and fires, they were also in the process of developing the services their growing town and families needed: churches, schools and health care.

Churches

> "The first place of meeting, as a church, was over a saloon, with a Rev. Mr. Hunter, as pastor. A house of worship was erected but only partially completed just below the front gate of the Spear lot. The location was not satisfactory..."[44]

The Methodist Episcopal Church had organized with fifteen members in 1852 and nine years later had a membership of ninety-three.

NOW

THEN

The Methodist Church
Maple & Lincoln Way

Auburn's St. Theresa's Church. Dedicated in October of 1859.

Courtesy Placer County Museum

Other religious faiths were developing in Auburn during the 1850s. The Placer Herald of July 16, 1859, printed the following notice;

> "Father Gallagher will hold service of the Catholic Church at the Court House to-morrow at half-past ten o'clock and will also preach a sermon."

Auburn's first Catholic Church was St. Theresa's and the dedication took place in October of 1859. The present St. Joseph's Catholic Church replaced St. Theresa's in 1911. From records concerning Aaron Bracy, we know that Father Quinn was in the Auburn area in early 1858. Father Walsh writes,

> "In these two years (1856 or 1857) Father John Quinn, the pastor in Sacramento, came up as far as Folsom to conduct services, but in December, 1858 extended his ministrations to Auburn..."[45]

Churches were developing and as the numbers of families increased, schools in the area became a necessity.

Schools

> "Public School in Auburn — The Placer Press says the District School in the Masonic Hall, Auburn, under the management of Henry E. Force, Esq., is meeting with the liberal support which it deserves. The attendance has more than doubled since the opening of the school, and is daily increasing. We are informed by Mr. Force that the children arriving show a neglect in the matter of education truly deplorable."
>
> *Daily Alta California, June 4, 1855*

There is conflict in local information concerning the "first" school in Auburn. It may have been established in 1851 or 1852 and located where the Shanghai Restaurant now stands in Lower Auburn. The first compulsory school attendance law in this country was passed in 1852 and one of Auburn's earliest schools was apparently a public school,

> "...run by a Mrs. Horton in a house known as 'parsonage' on the West side of Sacramento Street."[46]

California's admission to the Union in 1850 divided the state into counties and the counties into school districts. Funds were assigned for building schools, hiring teachers and for administration of these schools. Irene A. Burns, Auburn native and first woman Superintendent of Schools for Placer County (1914 - 1926) has written about this community's early schools.

A school district could form with just fifteen children in an area. The number of teachers hired depended on the average daily attendance of the students. Transportation was a major problem for the Auburn area. This became a community of one teacher schools with the teachers boarding with different families for a few weeks at a time.

> "Parents furnished the school supplies including text books. Slates and slate pencils were used instead of pencil and paper. The school room was furnished with some single desks but mostly double desks which could seat two or three pupils. The teacher's desk was on a platform in front of which was a recitation bench. There was an ample supply of blackboards. The school room was heated by a large cast iron stove in which chunks of wood were burned. A well on the school ground supplied the drinking water but in the absence of a well, the water was carried from a near residence. The water in a bucket was kept in the ante-room on a bench or at the well. All drank from the same tin cup."[47]

By winter of 1871, Auburn had 160 students.[48] A census taken by T. A. Wright, School Marshall, June 27, 1872, showed the following; of the children between the ages of 5 and 15 years in the Auburn school, there were eighty-five boys, eighty-one girls, two colored and six chinese and there were eighty-two children under the age of five.[49]

There was no specific curriculum in the Placer County Schools until the late 1880s and then,

> "The curriculum consisted of reading, writing, arithmetic, spelling, history and geography. Teachers were so rushed teaching all subjects in all grades they had limited time to dwell on comprehension which is so important. The beginners suffered most."[50]

There had been concern expressed in Auburn for a number of years about the need for a local high school or college.

> "A High School or College — We have repeatedly called attention to the actual necessity of an institution of this kind in Auburn. Our leading citizens here have talked of the matter occasionally for the last ten years, and at one time came very nearly going into the organization of such an institution, but again it died out as before and nothing was done. While our

The Sierra Normal College. Established in Auburn in 1882.

Courtesy Placer County Museum

people of this county are spending thousands of dollars yearly in endeavoring to give their more advanced children an education at distant institutions of learning, they have at home all the elements to richly endow and abundantly support one of the best high schools or colleges in the State or on the Pacific coast."

The Placer Herald, March 22, 1873

The Sierra Normal College was established in Auburn in 1882. The high school which came about in 1901 was an outgrowth of this private college. This school was then reorganized in 1914 and renamed, Placer Union High School.

The Placer County Teachers' Institute was an annual event in Auburn. Meticulous minutes were kept of those meetings which reflected the concerns of teachers in those early years of Auburn's development. Students' ideals was the subject chosen by the 1895 guest speaker from Stanford University,

> "...ideals of children change with their age...Girls generally choose an ideal on account of its moral character, while boys seldom do. Warriors, Statesmen, poets, actors and even pugilists are selected by boys as their ideals, but strange as it may seem, I never knew a boy to choose his teacher as his ideal..."[51]

It was the late 1880s before mention is made in these minutes of the need for regular meetings between parents and teachers. By 1896 teachers at the Institute were expressing concern about their attempts to introduce music into the school curriculum. Apparently local parents objected to this subject in the school and the teachers responded with,

> "...there will be times in the lives of their children when money getting will be forgotten."[52]

Health Care

Churches and schools were developing. It was now time for the community to turn its attention to health care services.

> "The establishment of the Placer County Hospital was not a spontaneous gesture of philanthropy nor an act of political theatrics but rather it was the end product of a logical progression of events as they occurred, plus the effect of the events of the times occurring elsewhere in the nation."[53]

Placer County Hospital - prior to 1920.

Courtesy Placer County Museum

The California State Legislature in its sixth session enacted a statute which lead to the creation of the Hospital Fund of the State of California. The monies for this fund were taken in part from the tax on all persons entering the ports of the state. In addition to the creation of this fund, the responsibility for the indigent (poor) sick rested with the Boards of Supervisors (Trustees) in the various counties. The organization of Placer County occurred with legislative approval in the spring of 1851. By 1855, Placer County found itself in the hospital business.

> "The first hospital, so called, was located on Commercial Street in Auburn...average census of this first hospital was eight patients per day."[54]

Auburn's founders were independent self-sufficient pioneers and their approach to medical care was to take care of their own. They wanted no interference from the government. They secured medical care by bid from private providers. The appointment of the first county physician was in May, 1855. Guidelines for this appointment were limited. The Act of March 31, 1855 (Article 3277) said only that the physician "was to be a graduate." A graduate of what was unclear until April 13, 1876, when the first statute regulating the practice of medicine was enacted in California. By 1860, the Boards of Supervisors (Trustees) were authorized to,

> "...establish county infirmaries for every person blind, lame, old, sick or decrepit in any way so as to be disabled and unable to maintain themselves."[55]

Placer County ended the practice of contracting for private medical care by 1873 and became directly involved in operating and staffing the county hospital. The Placer County Hospital, built in Auburn in 1900, remained in existence as late as the 1970s.

Auburn was changing. The 1850s saw social institutions develop and grow. Mining gave way to trade and commerce and Auburn became an attractive healthy place to live. Auburn's location, just above the heat and malaria of the Sacramento Valley and just below the mountain snows, gave the town creditability as a resort community. Not everyone visiting Auburn, however, agreed with its attributes.

The Letter

> "Auburn, January 8, 1864
> Over yonder is a glaring little Methodist church; a sprig of pine is stuck over the door, a melancholy pendant of the holidays. A little farther on is the church yard, grim and unadorned almost as a Quaker burial ground. And to the left, is a neighbor's house — tan colored — the idea of setting up such a vile

color right against the golden bars of sunset! Well, taste does not reign triumphant here...People go poking about with picks and hammers, and dig holes anywhere they please. This is 'prospecting'; and then, they never bury their disappointment, but let the great flaring cavaties stand about in spots, to the detriment of mustangs and other wild cattle.

Letter From Hannah Lloyd Neall"

Courtesy Northern Map Company

Auburn In The 1860s

Struggle For Law And Order

Early California mining camps sprang up fast and their populations were diverse and transient. As a result, crimes occurred regularly. Almost from the first, Auburn struggled to establish itself as a town of significance. There were attempts during these early years, successful and tragic, to stem the tide of lawlessness.

On the evening of July 11, 1859, George M. Martin, Placer County Deputy Tax Collector and former Deputy Sheriff under Wm. T. Henson in 1855 and 1856, joined Undersheriff George Johnston and Deputy Sheriff W. M. Crutcher with the intention of capturing an escaped prisoner and known highwayman. The three lawmen traveled up the old Illinoistown Road. About 9 p.m. they came upon two horsemen. Johnston recognized one as the sought after Richard H. Barter and called out for him to surrender. Barter drew his pistol. Johnston fired at Barter while Martin and Crutcher engaged Barter's companion in gunfire. When the firing ceased, Martin lay mortally wounded. Barter and his companion fled.

George M. Martin went to his grave at age 33 years leaving his parents and other relatives still in Tennessee. Survivors of the shoot-out described Martin's killer, Barter's companion. Martin's Masonic Fraternity offered a $250 reward for the man. No one was ever convicted of the murder.

What happened to Richard H. Barter? He was found dead the following day. His companion had escaped. Officer J. C. Boggs tracked the man. At a ranch, four miles south of Grass Valley, Boggs located only Barter's dun horse — with a bullet in his neck. After the gun battle with the deputies, Barter's companion apparently switched horses. The horse lived and remained in Bogg's care. George M. Martin was buried the following Wednesday at the,

"...old Auburn Cemetary with full Masonic Honors and...was followed to the grave by the greatest

> number of people that has ever attended a funeral in the county."[56]

Martin still rests not far from the memorial stone erected in May, 1969, for Richard H. Barter. Or as he is more commonly known, "Rattlesnake Dick." In later years an Auburn park, at the site of the shoot-out, was named in Martin's honor. The park is gone. In its place stands the Martin Park Fire Station at High and Hoffman Streets, Auburn.

Stagecoaches

Stagecoaches were vulnerable to gangs like Barter's. Gold diminished in the Auburn area. Some men chose crime as a way of surviving. Stagecoach robbery was one such way. This type of robbery occurred into the twentieth century. An article in the Placer County Republican as late as November 17, 1904, described a stage being stopped by a bandit between Placerville and Auburn, three miles east of Cool. The robber stopped the stage, stole the mail sacks and disappeared into the brush on foot. But, stages were not just for robbing. They also played an important role in the early transportation history of this area.

Early travel to the mines had been by horseback or by use of the Mexican Carreta, a two wheeled cart drawn by an ox or mule. This was a slow tortuous means of transportation which soon proved impractical. By 1849, John Whistman had developed a primitive form of stagecoach. He was using it over the fifty mile stretch between San Francisco and San Jose. By September, 1849, James Birch

> "...began operations with no better equipment than John Whistman; but Birch possessed far greater skill and business sense than his San Francisco contemporary...seated upon an old rancho wagon drawn by four Mexican broncos, Birch began his California career. He offered to carry passengers from Sacramento to Mormon Island, on the south fork of the American River. The fare thirty-two dollars or, if one did not have the cash, a couple of ounces of dust."[57]

Just two years later the Daily Alta California, San Francisco, November 12, 1851, describes Jim Birch as a,

> "...pioneer of that method (stagecoach) of travel and communication in this country..."

and the following is reproduced from that newspaper,

A tolerable estimation of the amount of travel between this city and the various mining localities and mountain cities of the region watered by the Sacramento and its tributaries, may be formed or inferred from the subjoined list of stage lines. For much valuable information on this head, I am indebted to Mr. Jim Birch, (as he is familiarly called,) who is the pioneer of that method of travel and communication in this country, and whose ups and downs over the rough road of California fortune would smash all the springs of action in men less persevering or unaccustomed to hard knocks and joltings. The following list may be of some use to travelers.

From Sacramento to Marysville there are six lines of daily stages. The Union Line (three old lines united) and three other companies with coach-wagon conveyances. There are three fine Concord stages on this route, and two omnibuses. Fare either way, six dollars.

From Sacramento to Nevada,	1 daily line, fare,	$15 00
"	" Coloma,	2 " " " 10 00
"	" Placerville,	1 " " " 10 00
"	" Auburn,	1 " " " 6 00
"	" Drytown and Jackson	2 daily, 10 00
"	" Stockton,	daily and tri-weekly 8 00

The stages out of this city are punctual and regular in the hours of their departure and arrival, unless delayed by bad roads. I have dwelt fully upon this matter because these lines are an important contributing source to the prosperity of Sacramento, and because their flourishing existence indicates the great increase of business and travel which has taken place in this valley within a year. The stage proprietors say that this year has been a very profitable one for them, and to judge from the character of the interest which sustains these lines, and to look upon their crowded coaches as they roll along our streets, mornings and evenings, we are fully convinced that our proprietors are well paid for the part they perform. As I stated before, the number of daily passengers accommodated over the road between Marysville and this city, averages seventy each way. Other lines are proportionately well supported.

Daily Alta California, San Francisco, November 12, 1851

AMERICAN HOTEL,
AND GENERAL STAGE OFFICE
Fire-proof Brick Building,
AUBURN, CAL.

G. W. GAZLEY, Proprietor.

HAVING opened this fine Hotel, the Proprietor desires to return thanks to his numerous friends for their former patronage while engaged in the hotel business in other portions of the county, and invites a continuance of their past favors. The "American" is new, fire-proof, and splendidly furnished throughout in Parlors, Bedrooms, Dining room, and Bar. From a long experience in the business he flatters himself to give entire satisfaction to those who may favor the House with their patronage. The Table will be supplied with the best to be had in the Market. The Bar always furnished with the best of Liquors and Cigars; and the Beds neatly kept.

☞ The office of the California Stage Company is kept at this Hotel, where passengers can take the Stages Daily for Sacramento, Nevada, Dutch Flat, Iowa Hill, Yankee Jims, Forest Hill, etc., etc., and tri-weekly to Marysville.

Auburn, June 18th, 1859.—my.

The Placer Herald, July, 1859

The California Stage Company made its home at the American Hotel in 1859.

Courtesy California State Library

In spite of the hazards, stagecoaches met the transportation need of the early settlers. The stagecoach business expanded between 1852 and 1853. With the merger of several lines in California on January 1, 1854, the California Stage Company formed. Sacramento's Orleans Hotel became the headquarters for this new company which rapidly monopolized the stagecoach business. Their ad, in the City Directory of Sacramento for the Year 1854-1855, showed five lines leaving Marysville and nine lines leaving Sacramento each day, all using Concord coaches. One of the Sacramento lines went to:

> "Ophir, Auburn, Yankee Jim's, Illinois Town, Iowa Hill, Newcastle, Secret Diggings, Lynches, Half-Way House, Beale's Bar, Long Bar, Smith's Bar, Horse Shoe Bar, Rattlesnake Bar, Condemned Bar and Manhattan."[58]

To eliminate competition, the California Stage Company, who had listed themselves in their 1854 ad as "the most extensive and complete line of stages in THE WORLD," had by January 11, 1855, reduced their rates. It was now possible to

Concord Stage (at the rear of Freeman Hotel)

Courtesy Placer County Museum

travel between Sacramento and Auburn for $5. The stagecoach company remained solvent. It was one of only a few businesses untroubled by the financial panic of 1855. Stagecoach travel further reduced California's inland isolation.

California's history is filled with tales of robbery and romance during the days of the horse drawn chariots of the foothills. Whether stagecoach, carriage or wagon, this type of transportation had its problems for traveler, driver and horse. The following article appeared in the Sacramento Daily Union on September 6, 1869:

> "On Monday as D. W. Parkhurst, freight agent of the Central Pacific Railroad Company and H. Morris, of the firm of Welter and Morris, were driving down the road from Lake Tahoe, they met with a most frightful accident. They were driving on a slow trot and when about to cross what is known as Record's log-slide they noticed a log just starting at the head of the slide. It was too late then to stop or in fact to think of doing anything, for, although the log had nearly twelve hundred feet to slide before it reached the road, the horses had hardly made a step before they were struck by it. From appearances the log must have passed just as the horses had got their front legs across the slide, and striking them swung both the horses and the carriage around lengthwise with the slide. Both the men were thrown out on opposite sides of the carriage, but escaped without injury...the gentlemen in the carriage were certainly fortunate to escape with their lives."

California and Auburn were experiencing rapid changes during the 1860s and methods of transportation were changing just as fast. The California Stage Company began disposing of its lines by 1860 but kept three: Sacramento, Folsom and Marysville. The Sacramento line went to and through Auburn to Nevada City. This continued to strengthen Auburn's position as a trade and commerce center.

The Pony Express

The Pony Express now made its dramatic but brief entrance into California's history. It had taken from six to eight months for immigrants like the New York Volunteers to travel around Cape Horn only fourteen years earlier. The first Pony Express ride began April 3, 1860, in Saint Joseph, Missouri, and ended just ten days later in Sacramento, California. They were later able to reduce this 2,000 mile trip to eight days. The riders were limited in the amount they could carry — only twenty pounds. It was also an expensive method of transportation — $2 per half an ounce of mail. The coming of the transcontinental telegraph in 1861 spelled the doom of the Pony Express and by October 26, 1861, it was over. But, the Pony Express is still remembered as an exciting moment in the west's history.[59]

The Railroad

The Sacramento Valley Railroad was completed on February 3, 1856, three years after the United States Congress authorized the survey for the transcontinental railroad route to the Pacific. This new line ran from Sacramento to Folsom.

> "Immediately upon completion of the road to Folsom...a demand for its extension was made by the people of Placer."[60]

Although all concerned had planned that the "extension" of the Sacramento, Placer and Nevada Railroad would come into the center of Auburn,

> "September 20, 1862, the road was completed and put in operation to Auburn Station, thirteen miles from Folsom, and six miles from Auburn...A busy little village grew up around the station..."[61]

The Auburn Station (probably located in the area of King and Brennan Roads, Newcastle) ceased to exist once the Central Pacific Railroad came to the area. There was a member of that early line who was to play a special role in the history of western railroading.

Theodore D. Judah, a construction engineer, had come west in 1854 to work for L. L. and J. F. Robinson. They were the builders of California's first railroad — the Sacramento Valley Railroad. Judah's fascination with the development of a transcontinental railroad led him to join with Dr. D. W. Strong of Dutch Flat in 1859 to begin the search for a passage across the summit. Dr. Strong hoped to divert some of the overland traffic from the established routes to Dutch Flat. What they found was the ten year old Donner Party route that was,

> "...a natural grade down a continuous ridge all the way from the Summit to the Sacramento Valley..."[62]

The Robinsons became aware of Judah's plans and he was terminated from the Sacramento Valley Railroad. This act left Judah free to pursue what was to later become the Central Pacific Railroad.[63]

Ground breaking for the new railroad was in Sacramento on January 8, 1863, and by June, 1864, it had reached Newcastle. There it was delayed.

> "Labor was a serious problem and when the track reached Newcastle, thirty-one miles out from Sacramento, Chinamen were imported, large numbers being kept busy until the road was finished."[64]

The Chinese

Chinese were at first welcomed to California and many came for the very same reasons as other immigrants.

> "The American People are the richest in the world. They welcome the Chinese. When you arrive in the United States, you will live in big houses, receive very high wages, have good food and nice clothes..."[65]

This was a typical propaganda poster in China in the mid-1850s.

Life was difficult in China during the 1840s and 1850s. There was the importation of opium, monies which had to be paid to foreign governments, wars, natural disasters and corrupt local government. It is no wonder the people were swayed with such a glowing picture of life in America.

While the Chinese yearned for a better life, they were faced with China's long standing policy prohibiting emigration. Part of that prohibition was political and a part based upon the Chinese tradition of not leaving "parents, family and the tombs of one's ancestors..."[66]

The Chinese did come to California in the 1850s and found it was not as those posters had promised. They did not spend their money in the local markets and began to fall from favor with the larger white communities. Also, mining began to diminish which put white miners in competition with the Chinese and other foreign born miners. Expression of anti-Chinese sentiments came as a tax placed on "alien" miners. This tax applied to all Chinese — miner and non-miners alike.[67] They had no voice in the courts since they were bound by the same non-white disqualification of testimony as Blacks. The amendment to that law of 1863 did not change the status of the Chinese in the California courts.

As surface mining was further decreased, first by the heavy rains and then drought of the early 1860s, it was necessary for the Chinese to seek other jobs. How different history would have been if Charles Crocker had not decided to try those small frail looking men from China as railroad laborers at Newcastle in 1864.

The Union Pacific Railroad coming from the East had ready access to European immigrants and material resources. With the Central Pacific Railroad, labor was always a problem. The white laborers were

> "...self-reliant, self-sufficient and free spending. They did not like the hardships and highly disciplined life of the railroad work."[68]

Whenever possible the white laborers went to the mines. The railroad had tried other ways of securing laborers and had failed, including attempts to use Confederate soldiers. Public opposition effectively blocked the attempt to use Mexican "peons." The only remaining alternatives were the Chinese.

"Old Chinese Houses built in fifties & still used. Auburn, CA 1935."

Courtesy California State Library

Chinese Laundries, Old Town

Courtesy State Historical Resources Commission

The eleven month delay at Newcastle was a time of decision for Crocker. The Irish laborers were demanding more money. In desperation he directed his superintendent, James Strobridge to go into Auburn and hire Chinese. These first fifty Chinese proved so successful many thousand more were hired over the next few years.

More and more white laborers were lured away from the railroad by the silver and quartz mines — more and more Chinese came to America specifically to work on the railroad. Not all came of their own volition. There were known kidnappings.[69] Once here, life was extremely difficult for these men.

The climate, food and language all presented problems to the newly arrived Chinese immigrants. They worked from sunrise to sunset for $1 a day in swamps, deserts and freezing cold. They imported their food through the Sisson & Crocker Company and were charged double price. By June, 1867, the Chinese managed to organize a one week strike with simple demands; they wanted higher wages, freedom to leave the railroad and seek work elsewhere and Charles Crocker was to "stop the Whippings."[70] Crocker easily broke the strike by withholding pay and food from the Chinese.

The Chinese conquered two of the most difficult obstacles facing the building of the Central Pacific Railroad: snow and tunneling. After meeting the Union Pacific Railroad at Promontory Summit on May 10, 1869, many of these Chinese laborers were faced with walking the eight hundred miles back to San Francisco. The Chinese survived the trials of the railroad because of their Confucian traditions, clean habits, insistence on food that was acceptable to them and boiled water for their tea. The "Six Companies," Chinese organizations of the time, have been described by some as exploitative of the Chinese in California. They did, however, offer a support system to their countrymen in a hostile land.[71]

Once their work on the railroad was completed, the Chinese workers found jobs as fruit pickers, ditch diggers, miners and domestics. They capitalized on the two chores most dreaded by the white population; the Chinese opened laundries and restaurants. They continued to face hostility and abuse and had to wait until 1900 before their children could attend public school in California. T. A. Wright, however, listed two Chinese children attending the Auburn school in 1871.

> "The complete development of the American West could not
> have been achieved without the railroads...and the railroads
> were completed because of American boldness and Chinese
> endurance."[72]

On May 13, 1865, the Central Pacific Railroad came to Auburn. There is an interesting but unverified first hand account of an early train wreck at Auburn. Fulton writes,

> "One of the first locomotive engineers lost his life in a wreck
> at Auburn. His infant son was adopted by Uncle Mark Hopkins

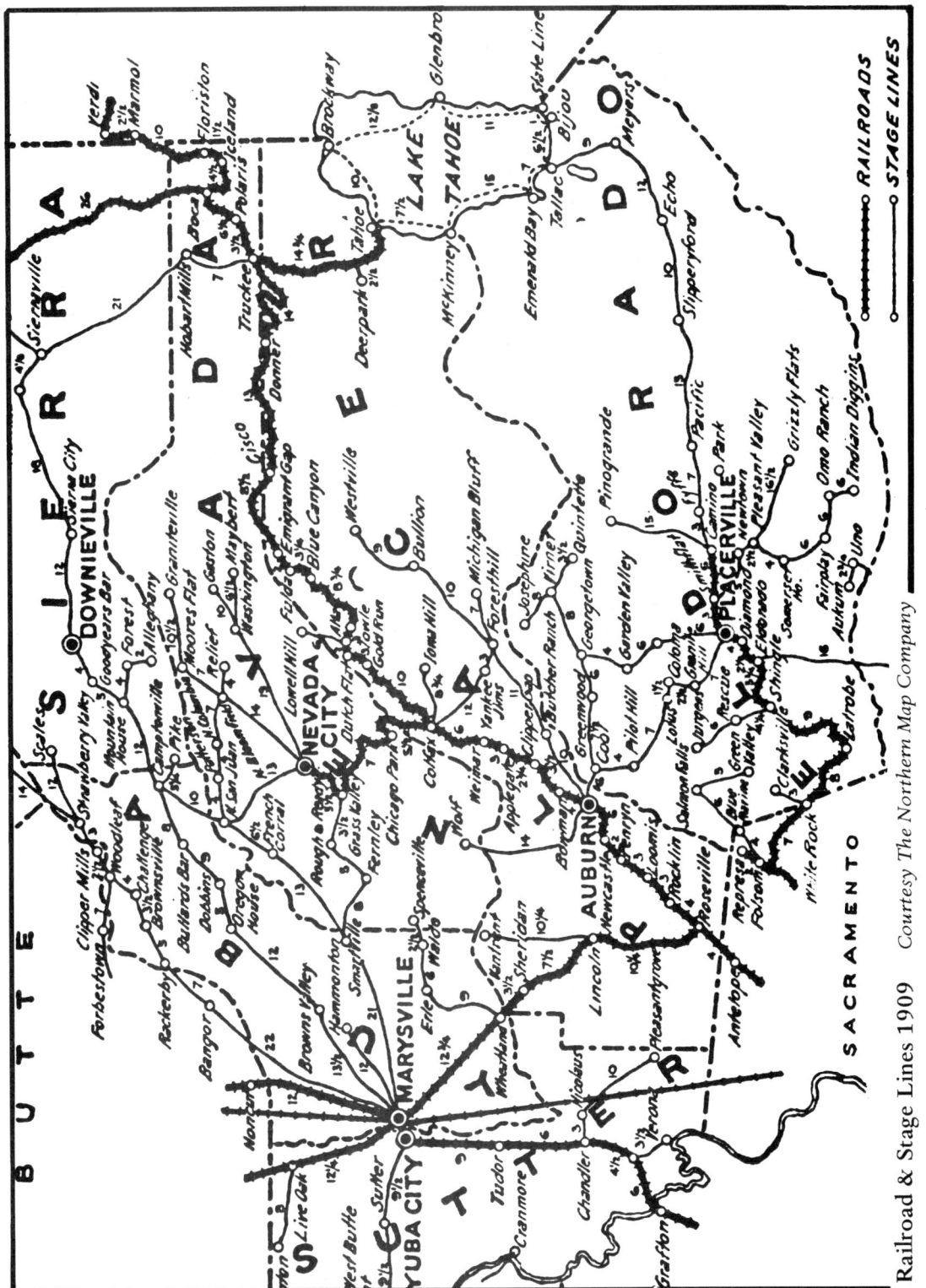

Railroad & Stage Lines 1909   Courtesy The Northern Map Company

Auburn Depot after 1865. *Courtesy The Huntington Library*

and his wife, who gave him all the advantages that belong to wealth and station, so that today he is one of San Francisco's leading financiers and one of California's eminent citizens."[73]

A small community of businesses grew up around this new depot just as it had around the old Auburn Station. Just four years after the arrival of that first train in 1865 this depot was the scene of an historic event for Auburn.

The Trip East

There must have been a feeling of excitement that Thursday, September 16, 1869, when the small group of California's 49er Pioneers, waited in the Auburn depot for the special Excursion Train to arrive from Sacramento. In just seven days they would travel across a country that had taken them, like J. R. Crandall, months to cross only twenty years earlier.

The train, picking up pioneers en route, remained in Sacramento an extra day. This allowed the Pullman Cars to be attached. Now the one hundred and fifty

Union, Sacramento, September 15, 1869

"Following is a list of the Pioneers who leave the city to-morrow on the excursion to the East."

James McClatchy, Sacramento.
Albert Leonard, Sacramento.
A. D. Patterson, Sacramento.
William Cummings and wife, Sacramento.
James W. Coffroth and wife, Sacramento.
Jesse Morrill and son, Sacramento.
Benjamin Bates, Sacramento.
Joseph Harris, Sacramento,
Wm. M. Siddons, Sacramento.
A. C. Sweetser and wife, Sacramento.
Wm. Mace, wife and children, Sacramento.
Mrs. Dr. G. J. Phelan and children, Sacramento.
Asa P. Andrews, Sacramento.
W. F Knox and wife. Sacramento.
Mrs. E. Wadsworth, Sacramento.
William Johnston, Sacramento.
B. F. Howard, Sacramento,
Wm. G. English, Sacramento.
T. M Gregory, Sacramento.
Captain E. D. Ebiland, Sacramento.
Henry Dalrymple, Sacramento.
D. D. Satterfield, Sacramento.
R. Butterfield, Sacramento.
W L. Everett, Sacramento.
E. F. Aiken and wife, Sacramento.
Captain J. A. Ellison, Sacramento.
James Lansing, Sacramento.
John Richards and wife, Sacramento.
John F. O'Brvon, Sacramento.
W. B. Freeman, Sacramento.
W. C. Felch, Sacramento.
Chas. D. Carter, wife and sons, San Francisco.
I. B. Purdy, San Francisco.
Samuel C. Gray, San Francisco.
Elwin Miller, San Francisco.
Dr. S. R Harris, San Francisco.
Henry H. Ellis, San Francisco.
Thomas P. Dougherty, San Francisco.
Wm. A. Dunbar, San Francisco.
V. Bruce Gates, San Francisco.
Captain Wm. T. Sayward, San Francisco.
C. C. Butler and wife, San Francisco.
D. E. Root and wife, San Francisco.
Mrs. Captain DeWolfe, San Francisco.
William S. Cook, San Francisco.
George Sawyer, San Francisco.
John A. Biner, San Francisco.
Mrs. Charles L Parent, San Francisco.
Peter Craig and son, San Francisco.
C. D. O'Sullivan and wife, San Francisco.
Robert White, San Francisco.
William Martin, San Francisco.
John W. Ackerson, San Francisco.
William H Smith, San Francisco.
Samuel C. Harding, San Francisco.
John F. Killian, San Francisco.
Wm. N. Wade, San Francisco.
James T. Bennett, San Francisco.
Captain Frank Johnson, San Francisco.
John Grant, San Francisco.
A. S. Peterson and wife, San Francisco.
Philo White, San Francisco.
S. D. Cunningham, San Francisco.
Atkins Massey, San Francisco.
Dr. J. M. Tewksbury, San Francisco.
Cornelius Storm, San Francisco.
J. R. Batchelder, San Francisco.
W. W Haney, wife and child, San Francisco.
J. W. Tucker, San Francisco.
Lorenzo Hubbard, San Francisco.
David Norris, San Francisco.
W P. Fuller, wife and children, San Francisco.
J. I Spear, Jr., and wife, San Francisco.
William Henly and daughter, San Francisco.
H. T. Holmes and wife, San Francisco.
David Jobson, San Francisco.
C. A. Litchfield, San Francisco.
E. T. Cole, San Francisco.
Ransom G. Moody, San Jose.
A. C. Erkson and wife, San Jose.
L. F. Sanderson, San Jose.
Charles B. Hensley, San Jose.
Samuel Morrison and wife, Santa Clara.
Henry Voorman, Alameda.
Henry Decker, Petaluma.
David Wharff, Petaluma.
H. A. Scofield, San Mateo.
D. W. Fanning, Stockton.
J. S. Haines, Stockton.
Mrs. Anna Votbe, Stockton.
Mrs Dr. Todd, Stockton.
William Saunders, Stockton.
S. H. Davis, Stockton.
H. Barnhart and wife, Stockton.
William Cantelow, Solano county.
Mrs. F. P. Burch, Benicia.
A. Powell and wife, Vallejo.
C. B. Houghton, Vallejo.
Judge Charles Lindsley, Marysville.
Newton Sewell and wife, Marysville.
Mrs. S. M. Hoel, Marysville.
Joseph Lusk, Marysville.
Captain S. B. Woodin, Auburn.
C. A. Tweed, Auburn.
Mrs. J. E. Hale, Auburn.
Dr. J. R. Crandall and wife, Auburn.
R S. Egbert and wife, Colfax.
Isaac S. Chiles and wife, Yolo county.
H. N. Cummings, Yolo county.
W. N. Brooks and wife, Yolo county.
D. Megowan, Yolo county.
William E. Wright, Yolo county.
W. B Campbell and wife, Truckee.
Daniel Willard, Placer county.
C. W. Smith, Grass Valley.
John A. Tyler, Grass Valley.
E. W. Hiller and wife, Martinez.
Samuel S. Turner, Tuolumne.
A. W. Oakley, Yuba county.
J. Q A Ballard, Placerville.
W. W. Brown, Elko.
J. W. Humphreys, Sutter.
Josiah Heacock, Ione City.

Courtesy California State Library

California pioneers could travel in comfort. Two great steam locomotives, Gray Fox and Aurora pulled the four Pullman cars. These cars included eating and sleeping accomodations plus two baggage cars.

The Sacramento Union of September 17, 1869, reported, that the day before, the pioneers had been summoned to the departure of the Excursion Train by the firing of fifteen guns. The departure from Auburn was not as noisy but no less exciting. The first change of trains, some 660 miles beyond Auburn, was at Promontory, Utah. It was here that just the previous May the Central Pacific and the Union Pacific Railroads had joined.

From Utah, the pioneers boarded the Union Pacific to Omaha with a change to the Chicago, Rock Island & Pacific Railroad to Chicago; then the Chicago, Pittsburg & Fort Wayne Railroad to Pittsburg and finally a change to the Pennsylvania Railroad to New York with arrival on September 23, 1869, at 6:30 a. m. These pioneers received much deserved attention as they traveled across the United States. It was an experience they wouldn't soon forget. The Placer Herald, November 27, 1869, reported that the Crandalls had a pleasant trip, enjoyed themselves well but that he (J. R. Crandall) had seen "no such country or climate as that of the foothills of the Sierras in California." The old depot is silent now, but there was a time when it was the place to see and to be seen.

Remembrances

> "The boardwalk of Auburn, the place to show new hats and dresses, was the depot platform at 4:30 p. m."[74]

This was one of the remembrances of Clarence M. Wooster who came to Auburn as the telegraph-ticket agent for the Central Pacific Railroad in 1876. The depot had been rebuilt after the fire six years earlier. Auburn was not a railroad town but it was growing as the center of trade and agriculture for the surrounding communities. Wooster remembered the townspeople coming each day to check on the train schedule and how he had

> "...boarded at Jimmy Borland's Auburn Hotel, close by. The main town surrounded the Court House down in a hollow a mile away...Grandma Crandall brought me books from her voluminous library and helped to acquaint me with many of the good folks of that very wholesome little city."[75]

Borland's Auburn Hotel was built the year after the Central Pacific Railroad came to Auburn. It was first called West's Hotel. During Wooster's time it was known as

Courtesy Lee Photography

"Recorded when Depot burned (1870) with Blacksmiths to right (now Auburn Iron Works)."

West's Hotel on Borland Ave. 1869

the Borland and finally as the Freeman Hotel. "Grandma Crandall" was Harriet J. Crandall who had come through the Isthmus of Panama in 1851 to join her husband in Auburn's raw mining camp.

The Crandalls

Harriet J. Crandall, born Harriet J. Russell on May 8, 1813, in Hoosick, New York, later moved with her family to Batavia, New York. After marrying John Riggs Crandall in 1835, they went to live first in Pekin, Illinois, and then to Peoria, Illinois. It was there they must have heard of the gold rush. In the winter of 1848-1849, J. R. Crandall helped organize and joined the Peoria Pioneers who made their way overland to California. As one of the developers of the Bear River Ditch System, he was working on this project at Lovell's place (half a mile beyond Bowman Station) when Mrs. Crandall arrived. Her first task was to "take charge of the Miners' Hotel."[7][6]

The Crandalls prospered and built a home in Auburn which was later moved to East Placer Street. With the completion of their home, Mrs. Crandall turned her full attention to the needs of her church and community. She devoted her life to Methodism. Soon after arriving in Auburn she helped organize the first Ladies Aid of the Methodist Episcopal Church. When the members needed a church, Mrs. Crandall helped raise the money. In the fifty-two years she lived in Auburn, Mrs. Crandall saw the raw and rancorous self-serving miners trying to strike it rich, families arrive, schools and churches develop, fires, crime, Auburn begin to move east and her husband active in politics. Through the years she dedicated herself to her church and community. Her obituary printed in the Placer Republican on December 17, 1903, best describes this pioneer woman.

> "Mrs. Crandall was a very exceptional woman...Intellectually she was shrewd and far-seeing and unusually active. She was intensely feminine in all the elements that go to fill out the meaning of that word; and yet she had a man's purpose along all the active lines of life. In the mere domestic manifestations she was entirely womanly."

Time Of Prosperity And Change

Auburn continued to flourish during the 1860s. The town had a railroad, churches, hospital, school and had incorporated. Incorporation had been discussed in the community for years — with particular reference to fire protection and street improvement. It was with the possibility of becoming a railroad center that incorporation was accomplished. By an Act of the California State Legislature, Auburn was incorporated on March 29, 1861. Ordinances were developed. Copies of these early ordinances were printed for the citizens in The Placer Herald. Seven years

Crandall Avenue appears on 1905 Map of the Freeman Tract.

Courtesy Placer County Recorder

later on March 30, 1868, the incorporation was repealed. Lardner writes that when it became clear that the Sacramento Valley Railroad would not reach Auburn, the citizens hastily concluded to disincorporate. Auburn remained unincorporated for the next twenty years.

Auburn was again devastated. By the end of 1861 it was weather not fire that damaged the town. The Alta California of Thursday morning, December 12, 1861, gives the following account,

> "Auburn Ravine is high enough to float the largest class steamboats and affords water enough to entitle it to be declared navigable for any size craft. Houses here in town have been carried off by the water and from all points we hear of immense damage having been done to gardens, orchards, farms, fences, etc., the like of which never was heard of before."

The Civil War was well under way by the time nature did such damage to the community. Auburn participated in the call for volunteers and the newspapers reported the war activity "of the East." By December, 1862, there were newspaper accounts concerning the California Volunteers as well as continued "Eastern War" news. There was obvious relief at the end of the "War of the Rebellion."

> "The news of the surrender (General Lee) has been received with acclamations of joy throughout the country..."
>
> *The Placer Herald, April 15, 1865*

The war ended. The Central Pacific Railroad had come to Auburn and the new railroad depot was fast becoming an important station. The 1860s brought increased activity by the Auburn community to develop a "suburb" around the depot. By 1870, this area had a freight and passenger depot, stable, blacksmith shop, hotel, stores, telegraph office, storage sheds and water tanks. All were lost in another Auburn fire.

> "At about ten minutes after 3 o'clock on Tuesday morning last, fire was discovered in the wood and wood-shed of the C. P. R. R. Company, and in the passenger depot and saloon of Curley and Mahon, at Auburn depot.
>
> *The Placer Herald, September 3, 1870*

The depot was a wooden structure; it burned rapidly. The people came from the main part of Auburn, three-quarters of a mile away. They fought valiantly, as always, to save the businesses. Had it not been for the Bear River Ditch running in front of Keeler's store and Wilson's Hotel, the "flourishing depot suburb" would have been entirely destroyed.[77] East winds carried the cinders as far as Ophir. These set secondary fires as they went. Railroad tracks burned and warped.

Fortunately the cars on the tracks were pushed free and sent rolling away to safety. Speculation had it that an earlier wood burning train had sparked the fire. Whatever the cause, the economic damage was high, "...leaving a net known loss over insurance of $11,355."[78]

Auburn had fires before and rebuilt. They did it again. The depot continued to prosper. During the next few years Auburn began its move eastward. These were also the years that Auburn would struggle, as would the rest of the country, with years of discontent.

AUBURN BUSINESSES ADVERTISE
The Placer Herald, July, 1859

WELLS, FARGO & CO.
EXPRESS
DISPATCHED DAILY TO ALL PARTS OF THE COUNTRY.

Gold Dust, Bullion, and Packages of every description forwarded. Collections, Orders and Commissions promptly attended to.

BILLS OF EXCHANGE SOLD,
PAYABLE IN ALL THE
Principal Atlantic towns & Cities..

HIGHEST PRICE
PAID FOR GOLD DUST.

The Express in charge of SPECIAL MESSENGER daily between Sacramento and Nevada via Auburn.

JNO. Q. JACKSON, Agent.
Auburn, Oct. 2d, '58, my

LOUISIANA RESTAURANT,
JEFFERSON HOGAN, - PROPRIETOR.
BETWEEN WASHINGTON and MAIN STS.

☞ MEALS SERVED UP AT ALL HOURS.

J. FELDBERG,
DEALER IN
CLOTHING, BOOTS, SHOES,
HATS, CAPS,
BLANKETS, SHIRTS, HOSIERY, PERFUMERY, &c.
COMMERCIAL STREET, AUBURN.

J. R. GWYNN,
VARIETY
AGRICULTURAL AND SEED STORE,
MAIN STREET, - AUBURN.

ORLEANS HOTEL,
MAIN STREET,
AUBURN, CALIFORNIA..

THE undersigned would respectfully call the attention of the Travelling Public, to the superior accommodations offered at this old established and well known Hotel. The House is well finished and furnished throughout, and the rooms kept in the best of order. The Bar supplied with good liquors, and the Table not surpassed in the country. Terms moderate, and every attention paid to the comfort of guests.

☞ Boarders by the Day or Week taken at the lowest rates.   JACOB GIBSON,
Auburn, Feb. 19th, 1859-my   Proprietor.

N. B.—The old customers of the House will be pleased to learn that Mrs. Gibson (late MRS. ELLIOTT), still assists in the charge of the Hotel.

DRUGS AND MEDICINES AND BOOKS.

NEW STORE.
DRUGS & MEDICINES
BOOKS, STATIONERY, ETC.,

FIRE PROOF BUILDING, COR. COMMERCIAL & MAIN STS.
AUBURN, CALIFORNIA.

THE undersigned having purchased the entire stock of Drugs, Medicines, Books, Stationery, etc., of Robert C. Hanson, will continue the business at the above stand, and keep as before a complete and fresh assortment of

Drugs, Medicines, Perfumery,
and a general variety of articles kept in the trade. In the Book Department will be kept a well selected stock of
Miscellaneous Works,
  Blank Books,
    Cheap Publications,
      Stationery,
Periodicals, Cutlery, etc,. etc.

The latest European and Atlantic newspapers and periodicals will be received by each steamer.

Those wishing to purchase are invited to call—it being the intention to sell Drugs, Books, etc., at the very lowest prices for *Cash*.

☞ Country Physicians will be supplied with Medicines at Sacramento prices!
        SAMUEL W. MORRELL.
Auburn, March 5th, 1859.—my.

GEORGE WILLMENT,

Cor. of Commercial and Court Sts. Auburn

WHOLESALE AND RETAIL DEALER IN

HARDWARE  **GROCERIES,**

PROVISIONS

WINES, LIQUORS,

Crockery, Flour, Grain, Feed, Oils, Cutlery,

MINING IMPLEMENTS, ETC.

Large additions are being constantly received to this already large and and extensive stock of Goods.

☞ Purchasers' Goods Delivered Free of Charge.☜

JO. HAMILTON,

ATTORNEY AT LAW,

(DISTRICT ATTORNEY FOR PLACER COUNTY.)

AUBURN, PLACER COUNTY, CAL.

Will give prompt attention to all CIVIL BUSINESS entrusted to his care.

AUBURN

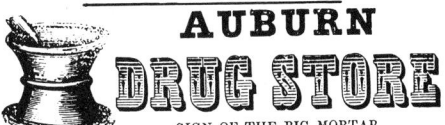

SIGN OF THE BIG MORTAR,

Corner of Washington and Main Streets,

Where all things pertaining to the trade is constantly kept on hand and for Sale, such as

Drugs, Medicines, Patent Medicines,

HAIR OILS and PERFUMERIES OF ALL KINDS.

PAINTS, OILS,

WINDOW GLASS, BRUSHES OF ALL KINDS, &c.

☞ Orders from the Country promptly attended to. PHYSICIANS' PRESCRIPTIONS prepared with accuracy, by

H. HAZELL, Apothecary.

GROCERIES, PROVISIONS, WARES, ETC

GEO. WILLMENT,

Corner of Commercial and Court Sts.,

AUBURN, CAL.

I HAVE on hand, and am constantly receiving large additions to my well selected stock of Groceries, Liquors, &c., at the old corner, consisting in part as follows:

Liquors.

Choice French Brandies;	English Ale and Porter;
American do.	pints and quarts;
Monongahela Whisky;	Piper's Heidsick;
Bourbon do.	Stoughton Bitters;
Holland Gin;	Hostetter's do.
American do.	Boker's do.
Club House do.	Lemon Syrup;
Jamaica Rum;	Raspberry do.
New England do.	Ginger Wine.

A General Assortment of Liquors; also a choice selection of Superior Wines.

Fruits.

Apples, dried; Peaches, dried;
Currants do. Cranberries do.

Miscellaneous.

Axe handles; Mustard, Eng'h, Soda;
Beef, dried; East'rn & Cal; Shovels;
Bacon; Mate es; Sugar, bbls. bfs
Butter; Maccaroni; and boxes;
Beans; Nails & Spikes; do Crushed;
Buckets; Nutmegs; do Powdered;
Brooms; Oysters; do Ground;
Barley; Onions; do Granulat'd
Candles, asst'd; Oil, Olive, Polar, do N. Orleans
Coffee, ground; Lard & Sperm; do China;
do Java; Pie Fruit, Eng. do Batavia;
do Rio; & American; do Manila;
Cheese; Pepper; do S.F. refin'd
Cream Tartar; Pickles; bbls. & bfs.
Corn green, tins; Peas; Tobacco, Grape;
Codfish; Pipes; do Peach;
Cranberries; Pencils; do Fruit;
Chicken roast; Pick handles; do Watson's;
Corn meal; Pork, clear and do Smoking;
Camphene; mess; do Nat'l leaf;
Clams; Pepper sauce; Tomato Catsup;
Caps, percusion; Raisins, ¼ and Turkey, in tins;
Crackers, soda; whole boxes; Twine, cotton;
do sugar; Rice, Carolina, Tacks, assorted;
do Boston; China, Batavia Tea, green, im-
Flour; Manila & Patna perial, & gun-
do buckwh't; Soap, Hill's pale powder, black
Hams, various; do. chem. olive Tomato's, in tins
Hominy; Syrup, Bost'n in Vermicilli;
Honey, in tins; kegs and bbls Vinegar;
Jellies; do S. Francis. Yeast Powders;
Jams; co. kegs do; Preston and
Lobsters; Starch; Merrill's;
Lard, in tins and Salt; A great variety
kegs; Strwber's in tin of spices and
Mackerel, hf. bbls Sardines ¼ & ½ bxs & case goods

Bailing Wire for Hay always on hand.

Auburn, June 18th, '59 – 1my.

Courtesy California State Library

Map of California (Gray's Atlas) 1873

Courtesy Lee Photography

Freeman Hotel, Auburn - circa 1900

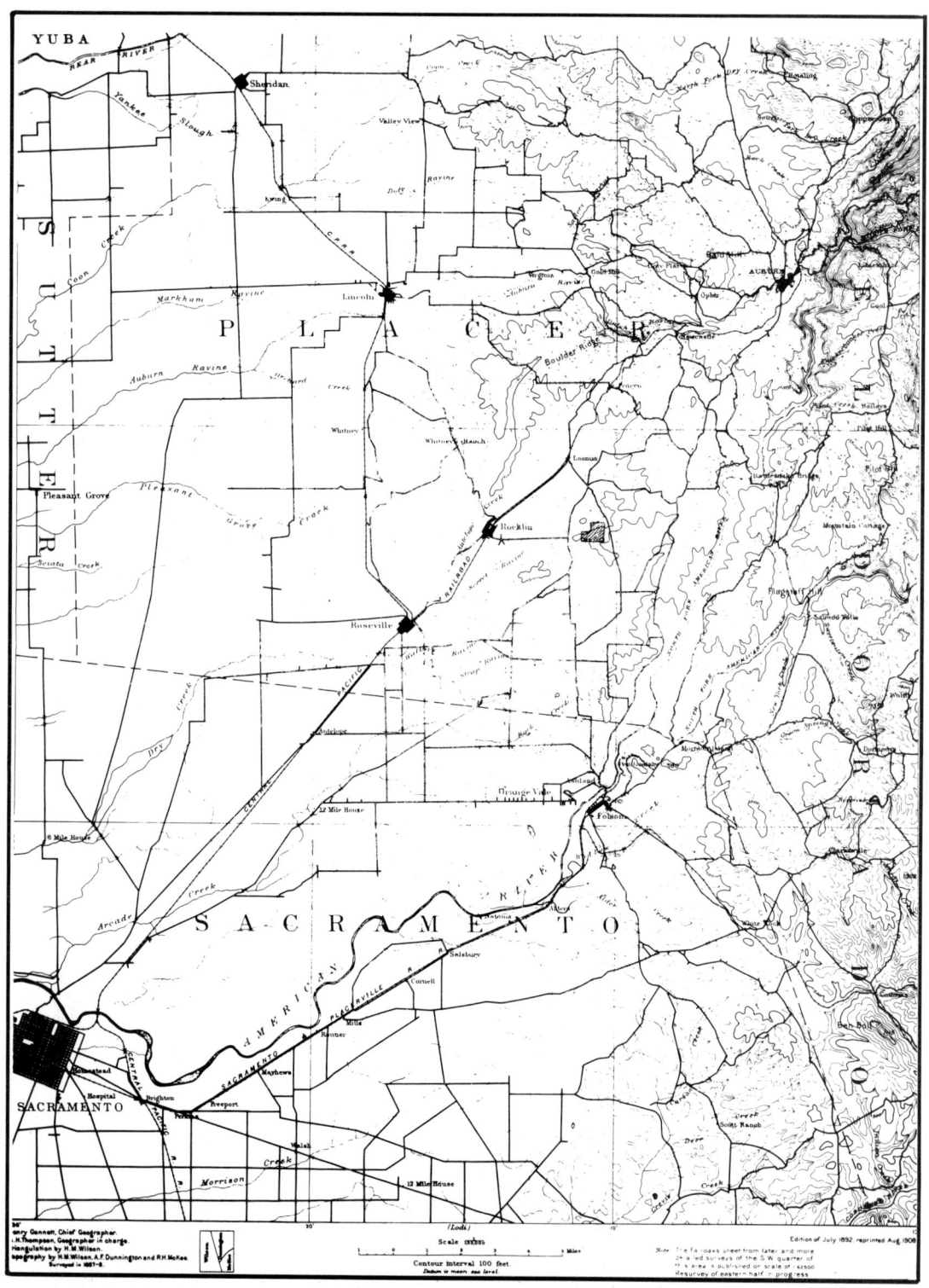

California Sacramento Sheet   Surveyed 1887-88   *Courtesy U.S. Geological Survey*

Auburn In The 1870s

Time Of Discontent

The seventies brought continued decline in mining in the Auburn area. Unfortunately, this decline came at a time when the community was still developing alternative industries. Agriculture in this area was barely out of the experimental stage. Although there had been fruit trees planted as early as the mid-1800s in Auburn, it would be the 1900s before fruit growing and shipping became an important activity. The 1850s and 1860s had been years of prosperity for California and small mining communities like Auburn. In contrast "a deep current of popular discontent ran beneath the whole course of California history" during the 1870s.[79]

The railroad had offered such promise. Now it proved to be as much a disagreeable monopoly as boon to the local economy.

> "...it (the Central Pacific Railroad) invariably refuses to pay its taxes (assessed property tax: $2,721,448) and never does without being compelled to do so by law."
> *Placer Weekly Argus, August 2, 1873*

The gold rush brought great numbers of diverse people into California. With the decline in mining, this population needed a new way to survive. Land titles were still clouded and public access to water uncertain. These two problems made it difficult, at times impossible, for men to develop their land.

Even before these difficult years, the continued immigration of Chinese was an issue in California. The Burlingame Treaty of the late 1860s, with its promise to place Chinese at an equal level with other foreign born persons in America, fueled the already smoldering rage. The result was violence.

> "In the month of July the Central Pacific Railroad Company began to receive hints of the organization of a band of desperate men, who angered at the action of the company in discharging white laborers from their employ on the other side of the mountains and substituting Chinamen, had banded together for revenge, which was to be achieved by burning and otherwise destroying snow sheds, bridges, etc., along the line of the

road."

Sacramento Daily Union, September 11, 1869

This group did destroy property at Cisco, California. With skilled work by law officers in California and Nevada, including Placer County's Sheriff Neff, the conspirators found themselves residing in the Auburn jail. Jacob H. Neff later became Lieutenant Governor of California (1899-1903). In 1908 he donated the fountain which stands to the side of the present Placer County Court House in Auburn.

Two months later John Stuart Mill (1806-1873), English social and political reformer, wrote to a Sacramento newspaper. This was in response to a question put to him concerning the issue of Chinese immigration.

> "Mill believes an overwhelming influx of Chinese might be injurious to the whites in several respects but that he does not believe such an influx is to be reasonably apprehended because as he said the Chinese who come here do not come in families not generally to remain in the country..."

Sacramento Daily Union, November 23, 1869

The rage against the Chinese continued. Southern California was the site two years later of increased violence.

> "The massacre of at least twenty-two Chinese in a riot in Los Angeles in 1871 represented the climax of...disgraceful barbarity; but similar incidents on a smaller scale besmirched the records of nearly every California city of the time."[80]

Auburn Continues To Grow

Even with these concerns, Auburn continued to grow and by 1875, was still described as a healthy area, "...above the fog and malaria of the valley..."[81] The town was beginning to feel cramped as Auburn's population continued to increase. The terrain around the Auburn Ravine had been acceptable as a gold mining camp but now it limited the expanding town.

> "The original location of the village (Auburn) was the ravine itself and the principal business part of the town is still there, but it has overflowed its former boundaries until all the hills in the neighborhood are covered with charming residences, surrounded in many cases by tracts of orchard and vineyards."

Placer County Business & Official Directory, 1875

By the time the Placer Weekly Argus published this directory in 1875, Auburn had:

five hotels (Empire, American, West's, Orleans and the Auburn), two restaurants, two dry goods stores, four groceries, two hardware stores, two variety stores, a livery stable, four wagon and blacksmith shops, one furniture store, one drug store, one bank, one harness shop, one meat market, shoemakers, tailors, barbers and saloons.

Changes In Mining

While mining was continuing to diminish in the Auburn area, the method of mining changed. In the mid-1800s the local miners had worked the rivers and bars in the summer months. They worked the dry diggings the rest of the year. The dry diggings began to wane. Other methods were needed. Hydraulic mining was one such other method used near Auburn, at such locations as: Bath, Todd's Valley, Gold Run, Dutch Flat, Yankee Jim's, Michigan Bluff and Iowa Hill.[82]

The shift to this type of mining is significant because it changed the structure of the mining industry. The early miners of this area were self-sufficient individuals who worked by themselves or in partnership with no more than ten to twelve others. They combined their efforts, shared in the profits and took on only a few other men in a service-for-hire capacity. While hydraulic mining required greater capital and a clear division of labor between owner and worker. Ditch companies and "holders of big hydraulic properties" began to merge.[83] Hydraulic mining, according to May, reached its peak in the 1870s. It was ultimately prohibited in the "Sacramento and San Joaquin watersheds after 1883."[84] Hydraulic mining became a major issue in California. By 1929 a survey was ordered to develop a method for restraining mining debris and a dam site purchased with plans for reservoirs at Folsom, Auburn and Coloma.[85]

Auburn Considers Alternative Industries

Auburn looked hesitantly at other possible industries during the 1870s. Refrigerator cars were just being used in the Midwest meat industry. These cars would be vital to the Auburn area's budding fruit industry. But, that was a few years away. The earliest record of attempts at fruit growing in this area was in 1846, "...when some peach and almond seeds were planted...along the north side of

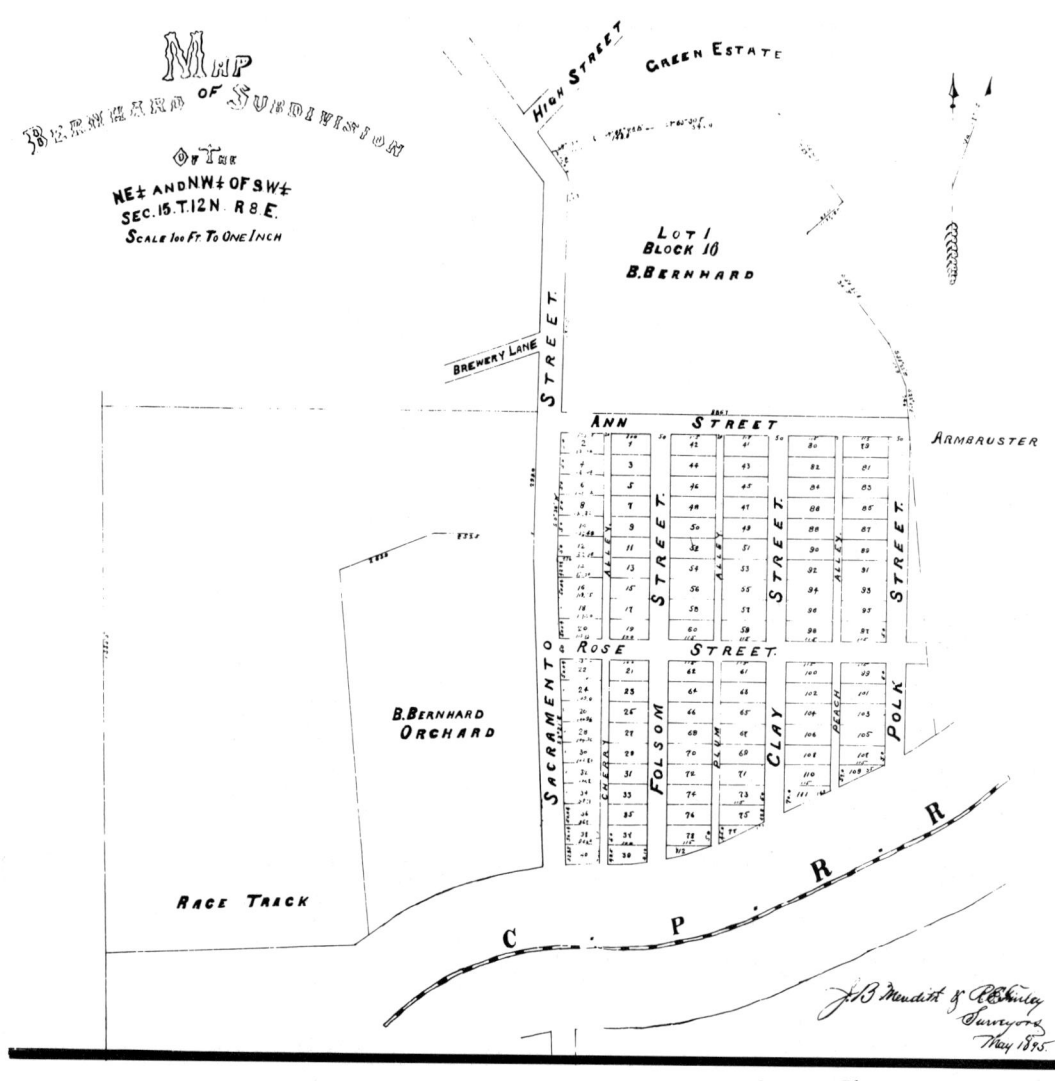

Map of Bernhard Subdivision, 1895

Bear River."[86] Those trees did well but the valley had most of the agricultural activity. By 1871 the,

> "...granitic foothills which border the plains were found to be productive...Barley was the first crop to be grown extensively in Placer County."[87]

The population in the foothills increased, irrigation improved and transportation continued to develop. By the 1920s the shipment of fresh fruit to Eastern markets became Auburn's most important industry.[88]

The State Legislature (1862-1863) enacted laws supporting silkworm culture in California. Auburn had the soil and climate to support this industry. It was also the type of work which could be done by the small family owned farm. The Bernhards were one such family.

Benjamin Bernhard came to Auburn in 1852 and, beginning in 1872, worked extensively with silkworm culture. With hard work by all of his family, Bernhard enjoyed success with this industry for several years.[89] Later, he bought the Traveler's Rest, a hotel built in 1851. In 1874 Bernhard built a stone winery which is still standing. This building, 291 Auburn-Folsom Road, Auburn, is the current home of the Placer Arts League's Gallery One.

Placer Arts League's Gallery One is located in the old Bernhard Winery.

Memorial Day Parade (moving toward St. Theresa's Church).

Courtesy Lee Photography

Historians have referred to the 1870s as a decade of dissatisfaction. The Hon. J. A. Filcher remembered these years as a time of change. Filcher came to Auburn, just after the depot fire of 1870, as Auburn's first public school Principal. In 1873, following the death of Joseph Walkup (California's Lieutenant Governor from 1858-1860), Filcher became owner/editor of The Placer Herald. He was active and concerned with the betterment of his community. His written remembrances, for The Placer Herald in the early 1920s, described his several campaigns for civic improvement. One of these encouraged the planting of fruit trees in Auburn. Surface mining was all but finished after the floods of 1861 and the drought which followed. Native trees gradually disappeared, along the railroad line, as fuel for wood burning trains. With this increase in available land, Filcher encouraged the development of orchards. The citizens of Auburn apparently did not share Filcher's vision. But, the residents of Newcastle, a nearby community, took the challenge and for many years operated a thriving fruit producing area. By the early 1900s, warnings would sound. These would herald the beginning of disaster for some of the trees so carefully planted in these early years.

A major difficulty in those early years for Placer County agriculture was the need for a viable irrigation system. The gold rush of 1848-1849 brought so many people into California so rapidly laws could not keep pace. Land titles remained confused for many years. With the change from mining to agriculture, water laws were desperately needed. Filcher wrote that there was no mechanism for public use of water in the Auburn area. A water ditch could not be forced through another's land. If permission was granted, the fee for such use could be exorbitant. Filcher described championing another community cause. He helped secure enactment of a law leading to public use of water.[90]

Auburn Moves Into The 1880s

By 1880 Auburn continued to be described as a thriving community with a train depot, three stage lines, a telegraph line and the construction of a fifty mile canal (the Bear River Ditch),

> "...to conduct the waters of Bear River into the town of Auburn..." was nearly complete.
>
> *Sacramento Bee, December 24, 1880*

This was the year that Auburn had its first Memorial Day parade. On May 30, 1880, Mrs. Crandall, with others, helped arrange the decorations.[91] The 1880s were also the years that Auburn continued to struggle with health and social problems. Typhoid fever and diphtheria continued as major diseases for the community; no one quite knew what to do with the "poor and homeless men" other than to jail them.[92]

The community began preparing for the "new agricultural District Fair," for

Placer and Nevada Counties. This preparation culminated in the 1889 Fair.[93] Strong feelings developed, apparently left over from the more unruly mining camp days, in opposition to horse racing. Ultimately, repressive legislation closed down many California racetracks. Auburn's track fell victim to the closures. Only the name Racetrack Street, near the present Auburn Recreation Park, remains to remind us of this phase of Auburn's past.

Auburn and the surrounding area had continued to grow since the summer of 1849. Thirty-one years later Placer County had a total population of 14,226,

> "...of which 7,125 were white males, 4,923 white females, 1,843 Chinese, 235 colored, and 100 Indians."[94]

Local Indians

Seven years before this census an article appeared in The Placer Herald of March 22, 1873, reflecting the community attitude toward the local Indians (Diggers). In 1871 the United States Congress had enacted the Indian Appropriation Act. This Act nullified ALL Indian Treaties and ALL Indians were made wards of this country. By 1881, Helen Hunt Jackson wrote the classic, "A Century Of Dishonor", which successfully mirrored her outrage at the treatment of America's Indians.

> "Auburn Indians — In nearly all the small towns of this county (we have no big towns) there are small bands of Digger Indians, who are objects of charity and commiseration. They are nearly all beggars, not thieves, but are contented to live from the offal of slaughter houses and decayed meats and vegetables from market stands. Their necessities drive them to debaucheries to get money that are demoralizing to others beside Indians. The men hunt a little and the women gather roots, acorns, etc., and they are all drunkards when they can get whiskey. The debaucheries of civilization they lay hold of and cling to as long as they can be reached, while for all the better characteristics of enlightened man they have no taste or even comprehension. The Indians of this county in 1849-50 were numerous, wild and warlike, but down they have dwindled into small fragmentary bands, and are almost universally pitiable paupers. Humanity and decency both demand that they should be taken care of for their few remaining years, for the day is not distant when all these Indians and their race will be numbered with the nations of the past. There are some twenty of these Indians at Auburn, under Captain Tom, a well enough disposed chief, but he cannot exercise much control

over them. They should be taken to a reservation and taken care of. The Government appropriates money enough every year to board all the Indians at first-class hotels, and it is as little as the agents should do, to come around and gather up these straggling Indians, take them off to some reservation and take good care of them. There are some well managed reservations. We think our people here would be glad to get rid of our Indians and we know it is the duty of the United States government to take care of them."

The Placer Herald, March 22, 1873

Auburn Recruits "Home Seekers"

The year 1885 saw the Placer County Immigration Society actively encouraging "home seekers...to this portion of the State."[95] Two years later The Placer County Bank was established in Auburn. By 1888 Auburn had daily postal service, a new firehouse at the head of Railroad Street (now Lincoln Way) and, on May 2, 1888, the city incorporated for the second time.

Although not necessarily the population the article (printed in The Placer Herald on April 11, 1885, encouraging "home seekers" to Auburn) had been addressing, by 1889 Japanese began moving to America's West Coast in great numbers.

Old Auburn Post Office

Courtesy Lee Photography

"Old Business Section of Lower Auburn"

Courtesy California State Library

Auburn Fire House at "head of Railroad Street" (Lincoln Way) 1890.

Courtesy Lee Photography

The Japanese

Japan's isolation, since the early 17th century, began to change only after contacts in the 1850s with Commodore Matthew C. Perry. With much the same experience as the early Chinese immigrants, those first Japanese, primarily laborers, were well received. They seemed able to assimilate into the larger American culture in a way the Chinese were unable or unwilling to do. Although the Japanese entered this country as laborers, their industriousness soon led many of them to become farm owners. This put them in competition with the Caucasian community. Antagonism resulted. As the Japanese prevailed in the Russo-Japanese War of 1904, antagonism gave way to fear. Exclusionary legislation followed, but,

> "With the outbreak of World War I, the need for agriculture labor and products became great, and in spite of the Alien Land Law (of 1913), Japanese participation in agriculture entered its golden era."[96]

This new era was in marked contrast to the agricultural attempts in El Dorado County by the Wakamatsu Colony in the late 1860s. California's response was positive to this small group of Japanese led by J. H. Schnell. The plan, however, to raise tea plants and mulberry trees failed. All that remains of that valiant group is the grave of "OKEI, died 1871, age 19 years, a Japanese girl."[97]

From eighty-six Japanese in California in 1880, the population increased to 71,952 by 1920. Most entered between 1910 and 1920. The Auburn City Census of 1900 places a single Japanese man, born in Japan in 1874 and immigrating to the United States in 1895, in Auburn by 1900.

As the soldiers began to return to their homes after World War I, and with Japan's rising nationalism, agitation against the Japanese was "reignited." The Japanese continued their agricultural pursuits. By 1941 they were raising 42 per cent of California's truck crops.[98] This fact again placed them in competition with the larger community. It was this successful agricultural competition which contributed to the pressure for evacuation of the Japanese in 1942.

If the 1850s and 1860s had been the formative and prosperous years for Auburn, then the 1870s were the uneasy years. Reliance upon a resort trade was not enough to sustain this rural community. Auburn struggled with its need to develop acceptable local industries at the same time many of its citizens resisted change of any kind. Mining, which had created Auburn, was undergoing drastic modification. Auburn's citizens faced two major problems: disappointment with the railroad and the Chinese issue. Those early settlers who had remained in Auburn were now, twenty years later, community leaders. They brought their skills, experience, attitudes and beliefs with them to their new home. These were reflected in the social institutions which developed. Life in Auburn became known, comfortable and secure for many. The local population began to stabilize and for the next fifty years Auburn would remain a close-knit rural foothill community.

Courtesy Lee Photography

Lower Auburn - circa 1900

Snow In Auburn (before 1911 - St. Theresa's Church in Background)

Courtesy Lee Photography

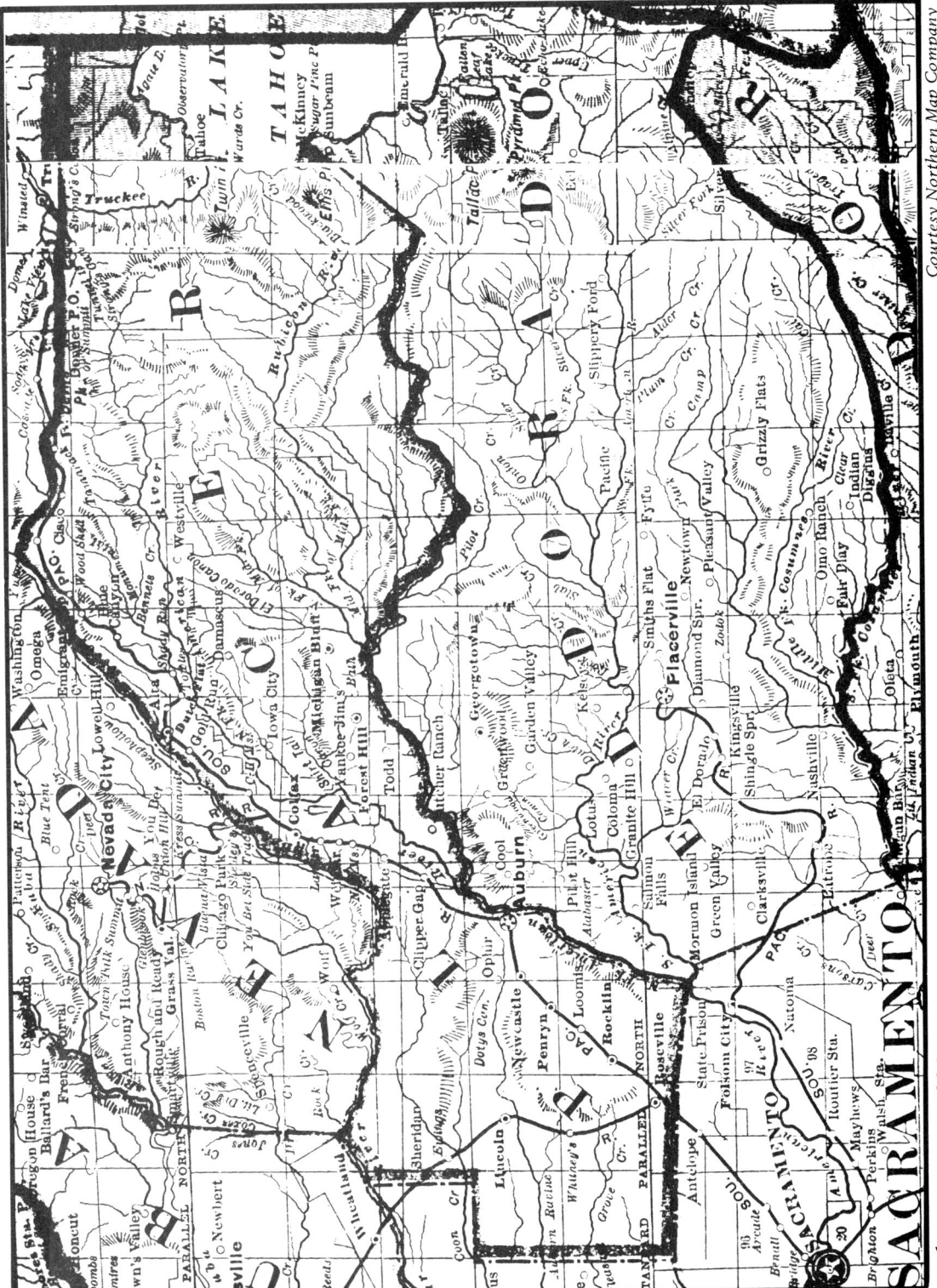

Placer County 1892

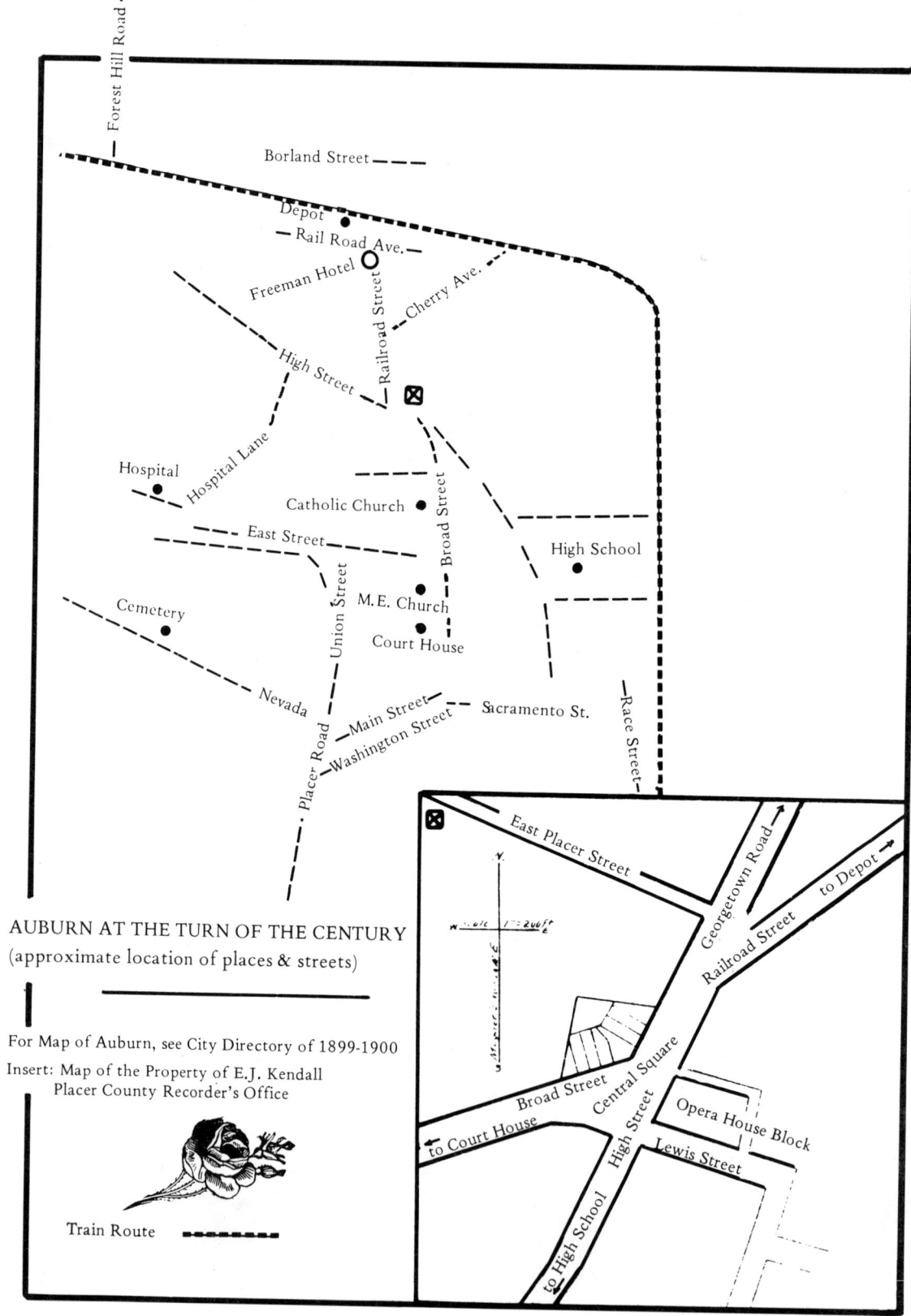

Auburn Moves Into The 20th Century

Culture Moves East

The Auburn Opera House was ready for its formal opening when the following appeared in 1891,

> "...the county seat (Auburn)...had attained considerable reputation as a health resort...the Court House and county offices are old buildings that have done duty for many years...within the town is a well-appointed county hospital. On one of the hills overlooking the town is the Sierra Normal College, est., 1882 by Professor M. W. Ward...a fine stone and brick opera house is now being erected at a cost of something like $40,000. Water from the Bear River Ditch...the pressure of water being sufficient to generate the electricity with which the town is lighted; but there are no manufactories to take advantage of this convenient water supply...Auburn is a shipping point of great importance, drawing largely from the sister county of El Dorado. ...there are two fruit-packing establishments at the depot." [99]

The motivation for building a new opera house, when Auburn already had one, is unclear. However, on May 6, 1890, the Articles of Incorporation of the Auburn Opera House and Pavilion Association were filed with the Placer County Clerk's Office. This Opera House was built on the "Lardner Lot" at the head of Broad Street with the Pavilion on the Lewis Street side. This put Auburn's center of culture further east than the earlier Washington Street facility.[100]

By eight o'clock Thursday evening, November 19, 1891, the Auburn Opera House had filled with the opening night audience. Threatening weather and unpaved streets did not stop the populace from coming to Auburn's grand social event. They came from as far away as Sacramento and Truckee. Over six hundred people crowded into the Opera House that evening. A third of them had come from outside of Auburn.

A special train from Sacramento brought Governor Henry H. Markham to Auburn for the opening. This added a distinguished atmosphere to the festive evening. New dresses and bonnets were the order of the evening. Flower decorations, from the chrysanthemum social held at the new Pavilion the night before, were provided by the Ladies Aid Society of the Methodist Episcopal Church.

The evening's entertainment began with the Auburn Hussar Band playing several lively numbers outside the Opera House before the performance began.

> "The performance opened up with a selection by the Newcastle Orchestra. They were reinforced by a drummer from San Francisco, and their playing was excellent, and added much to the entertainment."

The curtain rose on a one-act drama, "Sunset." The orchestra again played and then the curtain rose on "Dr. Bill." This comedy, in three acts, was without much plot but was "ridiculously funny in parts." This was followed by the much publicized high kicking "kangaroo dance." The performances did not receive rave reviews. When asked how they had enjoyed the show, the people attending this first night at the new Auburn Opera House were heard to say:

> "Well, eh, the building and the appointments were perfectly lovely; it is the nicest little theatre in the country."[101]

Many different activities were held at the Opera House, in the years that followed, such as the Temperance Meeting in the Fall of 1892. There was a time when Auburn had its own stock company. Famous performers graced the stage of this venerable building. John Philip Sousa was one such person. His stirring marches were heard one Saturday, November 2, 1907.

It was a stormy Monday evening on the 26th day of October when a poet came to Auburn as a guest speaker of the Placer County Teachers Institute of 1896. Joaquin Miller spoke on the "unanimity" of all the world's great teachers.

> "As all approach the light and truth all were so close together that they could touch hands. All taught the immortality of the soul and all taught the valor of gentleness."[102]

The Auburn Opera House is gone now. It burned on October 3, 1957.

Broad Street (looking East) Central Square & Auburn Opera House, pre-1900   *Lee Photography*

Courtesy Lee Photography

Auburn Opera House 1946 (Kenison Block/Building)

Placer County Court House (with bell) rises above 1850s building.

Courtesy California State Library

The "New" Court House

The Auburn Opera House had been a part of Auburn life for three years when the new Placer County Court House was dedicated. The old two storied wooden court house of 1854 had served the town well. The time had come for a modern structure. The new California State Constitution had redefined county seats and boundaries. By the late 1880s some of Auburn's citizens were considering a new building. Many people, however, refused to support the necessary bonds.

> "Finally the supervisors began levying and collecting a small 5% tax each year, and after a few years had about $27,000 accumulated in a court-house fund."[103]

Some members of the community complained that the building was not convenient and that too much money had been spent. The builders, however, had made good use of local materials. The granite came from Rocklin, the terra-cotta bricks from Lincoln, lime and lumber were secured locally and the slate for the roof came from El Dorado County.[104]

No dedication would be complete without a parade. Auburn had one on Wednesday, July 4, 1894. It began at the Freeman Hotel and moved down Railroad Street to the new court house. There were speeches. They laid the corner stone containing a "metal casket." Deposited in this "casket" were:

> "One copy each of the Placer County Republican, The Placer Herald, Placer Argus, Rocklin Representative, Lincoln News-Messenger, Newcastle News, Colfax Sentinel and Sunday Examiner, a Public School Manual, the Great Register and a photograph of John C. Boggs, the oldest continuous resident of Placer County, a package of American gold and silver coins, a copper cent, a Canadian coin, a Midwinter Fair Medal, a Helvetian coin and a share of stock of the old Sacramento Placer & Nevada Railroad Company."
>
> *Placer County Republican, July 6, 1894*

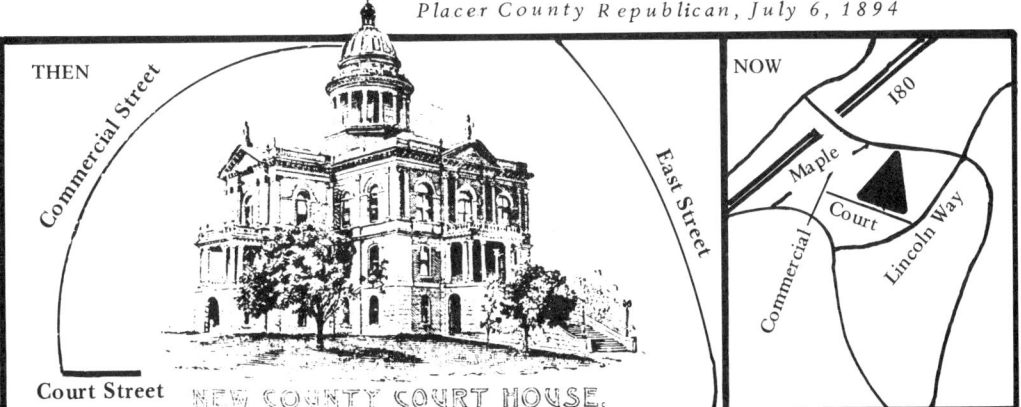

Labor Unrest

The summer of 1894 was the time of the Placer County Court House dedication and California's great railroad strike. Labor unrest had developed throughout the country during the 1870s and increased over the next twenty years. Auburn felt the impact of the strike that summer.

> "The strike situation remains unchanged. Not a wheel is moving between Sacramento and Truckee. Conveyances are passing through with passengers from Grass Valley, Auburn and other points. The early papers, mail and provisions are being brought from Sacramento by team. The strikers are hopeful and say they are sure to win."
>
> *Sacramento Union, July 2, 1894*

The strike interrupted the shipment of fruit in the Auburn area but there was "general sympathy for the railroad men." [105] The community was less supportive in the later years of the "Wobblies." [106] In 1905 Debs formed the Industrial Workers of the World (Wobblies) in Chicago. This organization worked actively with miners and migratory laborers in the western states. Eight years later the Wheatland Riot represented a major labor upheaval. Although in close proximity to Placer County, this riot appeared to have little impact on Auburn. Labor problems for Auburn were still a few years away.

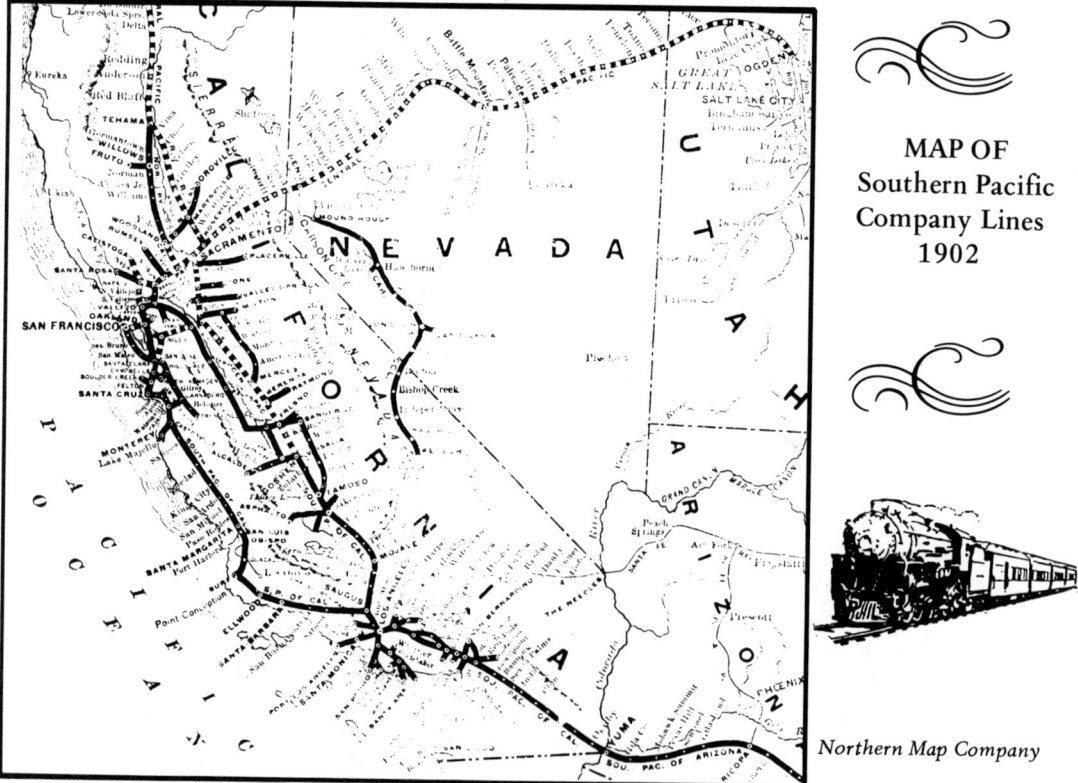

MAP OF
Southern Pacific
Company Lines
1902

Northern Map Company

Toward The 20th Century

Auburn insulated itself from outside disturbances during these years and its citizens continued to develop their town. Auburn had electric lights as early as 1886 and telephone service by 1891. The much sought after paved streets were yet to come. Now that the new court house was a reality, the town needed new ordinances.

ORDINANCES
OF THE CITY OF AUBURN.

Published by Authority of the Board of Trustees at a meeting on May 17, 1899, by a Resolution unanimously passed, Trustees J. W. Morgan Chairman, E. C. Snowden, W. A. Freeman, W. F. Wildman and Ed. Wooldridge, being present.

These Ordinances of the City of Auburn can be found in the Auburn City Directory 1899-1900. They represent the concerns of the times. For example;

"Ordinance No. 2   Adopting a Seal for the City of Auburn,

Ordinance No. 6   Providing a Revenue System for the City of Auburn,

Ordinance No. 8   Creating a Pound District in the City of Auburn,
Sec. 2 — It shall be unlawful for any Horse, Mules, Jacks, Jennies, Hogs, Pigs, Sheep, Goats, or any horned cattle to run at large or be herded or pastured within the limits of said pound district...,

Ordinance No. 13   Regulating the use of Cigarettes by Minors in the City of Auburn,

Ordinance No. 17   To Preserve the Peace and Good Order of the City of Auburn,
Sec. 1 — No person shall within the City of Auburn - 2d. Utter in the hearing of two or more persons any bandy, lewd, obscene or profane language, word or epithet.

Ordinance No. 43   To Prohibit Fast Driving over the High Bridge Railroad Crossing on Cherry Avenue Extension,
Sec. 1 — No person shall ride or drive an animal across the bridge over the deep railroad cut on Cherry Avenue extension at a gait or rate of speed faster than a walk."

"Ordinance No. 59 Establishing a Board of Health."

The Auburn Municipal Codes replaced these Ordinances and city government through the Board of Trustee system is a thing of the past. The ordinances were published in Auburn's first City Directory in 1899. It was with pride that the authors of that directory described the history and current achievements of the town as "...one of the most interesting small cities in the State of California."[107]

It was in 1899 that Auburn recorded a population of over 2,000, had five churches, daily trains going east and west, a sewer and water system, daily mail service and stage lines. Auburn businesses at the close of the 19th century reflected the diverse needs of the community. There were the usual hotels and saloons but now there was a milliner, plumber & tinner, architect & builder, and cigar manufacturer. Attorneys, druggists, barbers and blacksmiths continued to provide services to this rural foothill "city" as did the merchants selling groceries, furniture, hay and wood.

In the historical range experienced by Auburn since its beginning, the town welcomed the new century with the commendable and the tragic. By 1900, Auburn had a new Placer County Hospital. It would seem primitive by today's medical technology but the community put as much care and attention into the building and operation as was possible at the time.

> "The Board appeared to be willing to try the newest and the latest and to provide the best possible hospital plant they could afford."[108]

Increased health awareness came with the new century. Diphtheria antitoxin and a method for controlling yellow fever were discovered. Typhus vaccine would follow. These discoveries were not enough, however, to prevent a measles epidemic from closing the Auburn school in 1918. Nor did they stop the deadly influenza. By 1920, twenty million people had died from influenza in the United States. Unfortunately, Auburn shared in this epidemic. The new century also brought tragedy of a different kind.

An Auburn Tragedy

By the time the fire bell had sounded in Lower Auburn at 7:30 p. m. on Thursday, November 10, 1904, the Weber home was ablaze. As the local citizens battled the fire, they found the bodies of Julius Weber, a retired brewer, Mary Weber, his wife, Earl and Bertha Weber, their son and daughter. The first assumption was that the family had been overcome by fire and smoke. Facts later revealed they had all been murdered.

Adolph "Dolphy" Weber, the surviving son, was arrested and charged with the crimes. Auburn's most sensational murder trial began on January 26, 1905. Weber had the assistance of four skilled defense lawyers. Included among these was Grove

L. Johnson, the father of Senator Hiram Johnson of California.

It was speculated during Weber's trial that he had killed his family to conceal another crime. The Placer County Bank had been robbed in May, 1904. Weber repaid a part of the stolen money but he never confessed to the robbery or the murders.

In later years, A. K. Robinson, Prosecuting Attorney in the Weber trial recalled that after Weber's arrest there was a novel attempt to get him to confess which,

> "...consisted of covering a woman with a sheet liberally coated with red paint, then having the shrouded figure pass through the dim corridor outside of Weber's cell moaning ADOLPH, ADOLPH. Get out of here and let us sleep was Weber's only comment."[109]

Weber was tried only for the murder of his mother. On February 22, 1905, he was convicted of that murder from circumstantial evidence. The trial had involved many of Auburn's citizens. All had their opinions of the circumstances of the crimes and the guilt or innocence of Weber.

Adolph "Dolphy" Weber was taken to Folsom State Prison where he was executed, but not before a final struggle to survive. The following are telegrams exchanged between Weber and his attorney in Auburn:

Folsom Prison, Sept 27
F. P. Tuttle, Auburn, Cal.
    Send me some word.
Weber

Auburn, Cal. Sept 27
Weber, Folsom Prison: Have
heard nothing from the
governor
Tuttle

Folsom Prison, Sept 27
F. P. Tuttle, Auburn, Cal.
Prevent execution, insanity
plea, anything
Weber[110]

Weber was hung at the prison on September 27, 1906, and pronounced dead at 12:25 p.m.[111]

Adolph "Dolphy" Weber 1905

To the end — Weber never confessed, made no statement, left no writing and did not express his wishes for disposition of his body.[112] By Saturday, October 6, 1906, his body was given to Cooper Medical College in San Francisco.[113] Dr. Frank E. Blaisdell, Professor and Chair of Anatomy, a "noted criminologist," took possession of Weber's body. Dr. Blaisdell planned to "keep the corpse for a year" in an attempt to determine the reason for such crimes. He did state however that Adolph Weber was not insane.[114]

Another Auburn Fire

While the people of Auburn were recovering from the shock of these crimes, another disaster paid the town a visit.

> "Auburn sustained a heavy blow last Saturday (July 22, 1905) when property worth nearly $70,000 vanished in three hours and a half in flames and smoke."[115]

Apparently this fire, in Lower Auburn, began in the two story Snowden Building. Even though the water pressure was inadequate to meet the demands of this inferno, the fire fighters worked diligently. The post office block burned. Crosby's Stables, the American Hotel, Empire House and Mrs. Keehner's saloon were all lost to the flames. The American Hotel had experienced three previous fires; this one left only the walls standing.[116]

Auburn Moves Into The 20th Century

Life in Auburn during these years was not all tragedy. There were good times too. The Freeman Hotel was a popular community inn. It had succumbed to fire in the early 1900s. With typical Auburn tenacity the hotel was rebuilt. It had its grand opening on the night President Taft was elected to the presidency — November 4, 1908.

Auburn had a library by 1909. Built as a result of Andrew Carnegie's donation, for library construction across the United States, this public library was located on Almond Street. The town would soon be invaded by three revolutionary inventions; motion pictures, aeroplanes and automobiles. It was the automobile that had the greatest effect in bringing Auburn into the twentieth century.

Courtesy Lee Photography

Placer County Bank (Lincoln Way) under construction 1912-1913

Freemann Tract, 1891

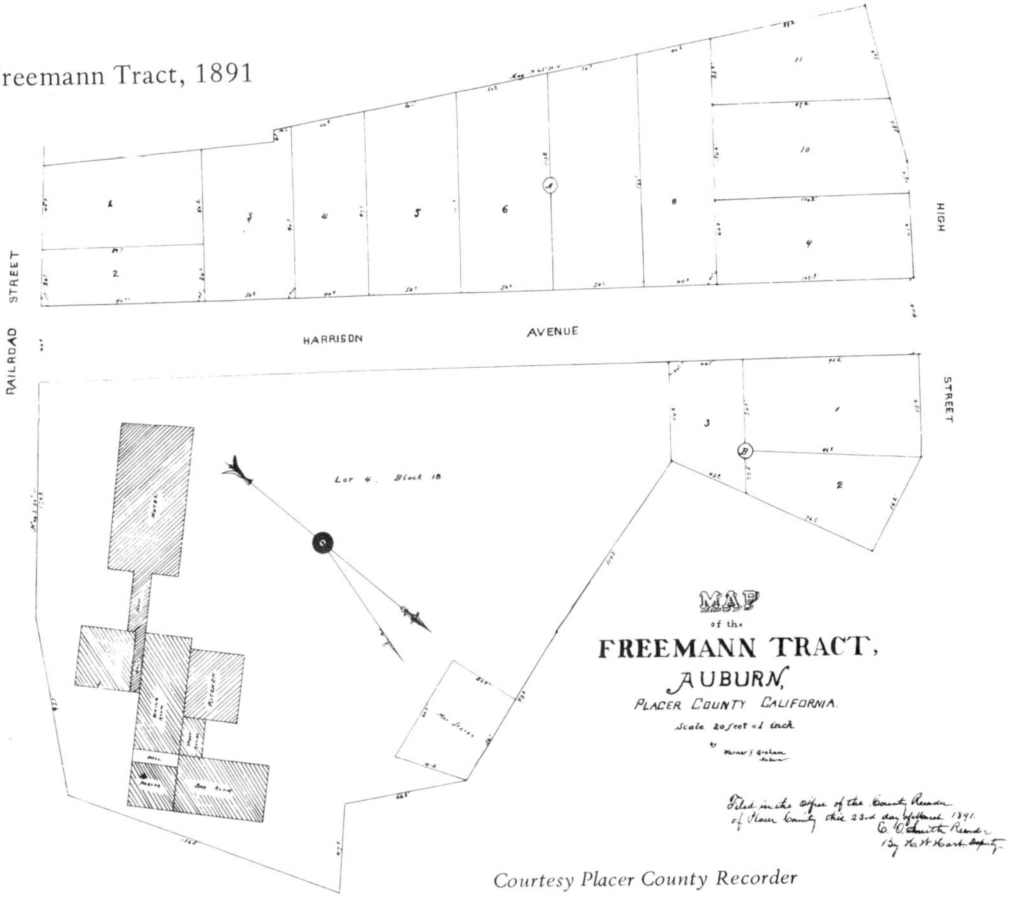

Courtesy Placer County Recorder

Freeman Hotel at Railroad Avenue, Auburn

In the first decade of the new century, Auburn concerned itself with local matters. Warning concerning "Pear Blight" began to appear. An agricultural disease that would, in later years, destroy untold orchards in Placer County. Another event in these years was a serious train collision near the Cherry Street Bridge. By November of 1907, the townspeople were considering establishing a second depot. This would accomodate the passengers and freight between Colfax and Rocklin. The plan was to place this new depot within Auburn City limits, on the Southern Pacific line and not far from the Odd Fellows Cemetery.[117]

Auburn had grown away from Lower Auburn and toward the East. This was over the objections of the long time residents of Lower Auburn. This new area became known as East Auburn. It was never an official name and caused confusion in an already scattered community. By 1911 it was time to name this new train station. The citizens of Auburn were concerned that the name selected, "...make Auburn ONE city..."[118]

Before the opening of this new station, there was an event in Lower Auburn never before seen.

> "The downtown section of Auburn was crowded Monday noon (May 17, 1909) with people from all portions of the city and surrounding territory. The occasion being an impromptu celebration of the coming of the first train down Auburn Ravine."
>
> *Placer County Republican, May 20, 1909*

This was not the train extension from Folsom to Auburn the community had hoped for in the early years. It was a train pulling a 70,000 ton steam shovel on temporary tracks through Lower Auburn. This train was taking the shovel from the Southern Pacific tracks to the Willits & Burr's construction site near the Odd Fellows Cemetery.

Not a town to rush, Auburn had moved slowly but steadily into the twentieth century. Men had come to Auburn Ravine to make their fortunes in gold and a town had developed. The town had not only developed but had survived to become a trading center of importance. Auburn's location contributed to this. People and freight had moved laboriously along the dusty trails of the early mining camp only to give way to the stagecoach and then the train. Now came newer and faster means of travel to and through Auburn — the automobile and the aeroplane.

Two views of the train wreck near the Cherry Street Bridge.

Courtesy California State Railroad Museum

Courtesy Placer County Museum

The East bound Overland Limited and Local collide at Auburn.

Courtesy Lee Photography

Train comes through Lower Auburn, 1909.

Fourth of July Parade - Freeman Hotel (in background)

Courtesy Lee Photography

The Placer Herald Building — *Courtesy Pete Hawkins*

The Placer Herald "sign" on display at Maple & Commercial Streets, Auburn.

Lincoln Way, Auburn (before 1911) *Courtesy Lee Photography*

Lincoln Way, Auburn (after 1911) *Courtesy Lee Photography*

Auburn Comes Of Age

Automobiles & Aeroplanes

Auburn was still using horses and wagons as the twentieth century approached. Those first automobiles produced by the Olds Company in Detroit, Michigan, were considered an expensive luxury. Some even referred to them as "devil wagons." By 1904, three hundred autos were registered in the United States. Four years later Ford introduced his Model T. The first sold for $850 but by 1926 the price had dropped to $310. California had 36,000 registered motor vehicles by 1910. Two years later the state had its first paved highway, "constructed especially for automotive traffic."[119]

The automobile gave people freedom to travel they had not had before. With this new mobility more and more people came to and through Auburn. The automobile, however, was not the only new invention changing Auburn's quiet rural solitude. Eleven years into the new century, the first aeroplane came to Auburn.

The Wright brothers flew at Kitty Hawk, North Carolina, on December 17, 1903. On September 11, 1911, R. G. Fowler left Sacramento at 6:00 p.m. in his aeroplane. He was on his way to New York by way of San Francisco and arrived in Auburn just 35 minutes after leaving Sacramento. Fowler landed on the outskirts of Auburn. The Placer Herald of September 14, 1911, reported that hundreds of people hurried to the landing place. Fowler spent the night in Auburn at the Freeman Hotel. The next morning about five hundred people came to see him take off. Fowler and his aeroplane made it as far as Alta, California, before colliding with trees. He survived but his machine did not.

> "Members of the train crew are said to have tried to literally carry away the wrecked machine in their madness for souvenirs and Fowler and those who stood by him had difficulty preventing it."[120]

The next year and closer to the ground, Auburn began to pave its streets. This was also the year California's women received the vote. The long sought after paved streets received more attention from the local press than did the new status of women. By the following year, a new invention came to Auburn — the movies. This brought Auburn still closer to the outside world.

"The Edison Talking Pictures will be publicly viewed and heard for the first time here at the Auburn Theatre..."

The Placer Herald, October 18, 1913

AUBURN'S AUTOMOBILES OF THE PAST

City Bus - 1910 *Courtesy Lee Photography*

Cars in Lower Auburn *Courtesy Lee Photography*

Old Car on Lincoln Way - 1913 *Courtesy Lee Photography*

Courtesy Placer County Museum

"Bus" outside the Auburn Hotel 1914 (once the Conroy Hotel)

Women at work in Auburn. Placer County Republican - circa 1910.

Courtesy California State Library

Women In Auburn

From the time of Mrs. Crandall's arrival in Auburn in the early 1850s, women had played a vital part in the creation and development of the community. They lived out their lives in the traditional roles of their time. Two years after receiving the vote, however, Auburn had its first woman elected to a salaried office.[121] This was also the year, 1914, that Irene A. Burns became the first woman County Superintendent of Schools.[122] Four years later, local newspaper headlines read,

Placer County Republican circa 1907

"WOMEN TO SERVE WITH MEN ON GRAND JURY
Thirty women and 30 men of Placer County appointed by Judge Prewett, Superior Court for 1918...This is the first time in the history of Placer that women have been called as grand jurors."[123]

This was followed a few months later with,

"WOMEN LAWYERS TO BATTLE TOMORROW...
...the attorneys battling over his (defendant's) fate are women."[124]

While some Auburn women were taking their place in civic life, others were being encouraged to leave town. Senator Edwin E. Grant had been diligent throughout California, for a number of years, in developing and carrying out his "Red Light Abatement Legislation." As a result of the Senator's investigation, Auburn's "women of the evening" began to leave the area between 1912 and 1918.[125]

Health/Social Problems

The new century ushered in exciting medical advances. Auburn, however, continued to be plagued with health and social problems in the early 1900s. A crucial problem was the community's water supply.

"Auburn's water is not fit for use during the months of May and June."

Auburn Journal, July 20, 1914

After many years of mining, the Bear River proved to be the culprit. Mining debris pollution became a heated issue in this part of California. A dam on the American River would later be developed to remedy the problem.

These years brought further involvement by the community in the Placer County Hospital. The years 1912 and 1913 showed 347 admissions with 271 discharges. The census on July 1, 1913, recorded 81 patients in residence.[126] By 1918 there was serious discussion about building a new type of health care facility. One which would house and treat tubercular patients. As a matter of public safety, the community voiced great concern.[127] The hospital was built and called Weimar Tubercular Sanitarium. Later an army hospital would come to Auburn which would capture the enthusiastic patriotism of the entire community.

World War I

Auburn moved into the second decade of the new century. There was more and more news in the local press of a pending war. When President Wilson finally asked for a declaration of war that would make the world safe for democracy, Auburn's men came forward. June 5, 1917, was the first local registration of men between the ages of 21 and 31 for active duty in World War I.[128]

Auburn participated in the war effort by sending men to fight, by conserving food, by adhering to two meatless days per week, and by being watchful for possible German agents.

> "Farmers and others are urged to be on the lookout for suspicious characters who may be engaged by Germany to destroy property."[129]

Community retaliation was simple and swift for those who offended during these war years.

> "A good deal of disloyalty has been expressed by some people and the community is getting tired of it...The names of liars are to be posted in the post office."[130]

In 1918, after a month of negotiations, the German government signed the armistice treaty. This took place at five a.m. in a railroad dining car at Compiegne. The war cost America $41,755,000. There were 130,174 dead and 203,460 wounded.[131]

By six a.m. on the day the armistice was signed, November 11, 1918, the citizens of Auburn, all wearing their required face masks against the dreaded influenza,

> "...poured out into the street...to the Freeman Hotel...marched to Central Square. An organ was carried into the street

Armistice Celebration in Central Square, Auburn, November 11, 1918.

Courtesy Placer County Museum

from somewhere and the musicians appeared with their instruments. An automobile served as a speakers' stand. From it Mayor M. D. Lininger directed the program."[132]

With the end of World War I Auburn again began to prosper.[133] There continued to be new, but less severe, flu cases. Nevada Street improvements began from the freight station to Palm Avenue and the new (East Auburn) Post Office began free mail. This last event meant for the first time in Auburn's history homes and streets needed clear markings. Labor conditions and the automobile made their impact on a time honored community business. Conroy Stable, Auburn's only remaining livery stable, closed. Auburn now turned its attention to new problems; the Great Depression and World War II.

The Great Depression

Placer Assessment Rolls of July 4, 1929, showed,

"City of Auburn: 880.22 acres
value of real estate: $467,470.00."
Auburn Journal & Placer County Republican, July 4, 1929

The month before this article, the town's lighting system, Bell Electric (organized in the 1880s) was sold to P. G. & E. By August, just two months before America was plummeted into the greatest depression the country had yet experienced, the following headline appeared in the Auburn Journal,

"FRUIT PRICES HIGHEST IN HISTORY"

Auburn had limited free mail delivery — limited to "streets having sidewalks."[134] There had been a telephone system in Auburn since the 1890s. By 1929, "Auburn had 811 telephones which was an increase of 76 phones in ten years."[135] By the end of the year the new Montgomery Ward Store would open in Auburn. The stockmarket "crash" came in October along with,

"BANDITS WARNED PLACER TO BE AN UNHEALTHY PLACE"
Auburn Journal & Placer County Republican, October 10, 1929

Sheriff Elmer H. Gum had just purchased a Thompson machine gun. Auburn was now prepared to face an uncertain and troubled world.

Auburn's citizens demonstrated the same pride and self-sufficiency during the Great Depression they had always shown by taking "care of her own unemployed."[136] An emergency unemployment committee formed by October 22, 1931. Some 104 names were listed. Of these names,

> "Thirty of the most worthy were selected from the list for work on the state highway on a three day a week basis."
>
> *Auburn Journal, October 15, 1931*

Highway construction was only one area worked on during these depression years. There were extensive city street repairs, including the improvement of High Street, under the direction of Chester W. Gwynn, Auburn's Superintendent of Streets.[137] Another project completed during this time was a comprehensive fire protection system around Auburn, for the town had literally been surrounded by a forest fire the summer of 1931.[138]

Fruit and nut values decreased. Shipping rates increased. The depressed years of the 1930s drove people back into the hills looking for gold.

> "Gold buyers in the Auburn district report more gold being purchased in recent weeks than for a generation past."
>
> *Auburn Journal, January 28, 1932*

If you had money in 1932, you could purchase Chevrolet's "Special Sedan" for $650 or a Conlon Electric Washer for $79.50. Or, you could take the fifty-eight minute ride from Auburn to Sacramento in the "automobile passenger stage." Once in Sacramento, you could take a round trip ride on the "Delta King" to San Francisco for $3.00; with your auto on board, just an extra $7.50.[139]

By the end of 1932, the Southern Pacific Overland Limited Train No. 28 began stopping daily at the Nevada Street Depot to let off passengers and pick up mail. A new unemployment camp, with capacity for one hundred men, had been established just outside the city limits on Forest Hill Road.[140]

Auburn did not move easily into the new age of welfare. This was in contradiction to the independent pioneer spirit of Auburn's early settlers. A particularly vocal group concerning this new era of "relief" was the local medical community.

> "Placer County Medical Society was one of the violent opponents of the MAA (Medical Assistance for the Aged) programs, as well as other governmental programs concerned with medical care."[141]

By January of 1937, the local "welfare load" had risen to 562 (persons receiving welfare assistance) and to 672 by October of that same year.[142] By early 1939 the community was warning "relief chiselers" that they were glad to have citizens report (illegal collection of relief money) any known cases for proper action.[143]

Unemployment would soon move to resolution. The community's future was brighter as diseases began to decrease. There were fewer typhoid fever cases and infant mortality was on the decline except in Placer County's Indian population. The community developed an immunization program. By March, 1939, there was a county wide program to vaccinate children against smallpox.

The year before, 1938, Auburn had three noteworthy events. The first was the worst storm in the city's history — up to seventy mile per hour winds. This storm caused extensive destruction of property, including tearing the roof off the "old" Opera House. The second was the dedication of the Auburn Grammar School. Thirdly, Auburn saw the passing of Chester "Chet" Gwynn.

Gwynn, a descendent of an early Auburn merchant, had been instrumental in having an Auburn park named in honor of George M. Martin. Gwynn held several important positions in the community during his lifetime. He had directed street repairs with "miles and miles of Gwynnite" and,

> "It was due to his (Gwynn's) activities as Chief of Police that the city (Auburn) was kept clean of slot machines during the period when slot machines were the curse of many other districts of the state."
>
> *Auburn Journal, March 10, 1938*

The year 1939 began with Culbert L. Olson becoming the first Democratic Governor in California since 1900. F. D. Roosevelt continued as President and Auburn businesses began to improve. This was also the year of the Golden Gate International Exposition on Treasure Island in San Francisco Bay. The Exposition's presence, so close to Auburn, represented a tourist potential for the town. Auburn had a new post office on Lincoln Way that would endure for the next forty-seven years.

The State Relief Administration established the WPA (Work Projects Administration) camp in 1938 on the forty acre Dorsey Tract near the fair grounds.[144] This area, known locally as "Camp Flint," was at first a camp of tents. Later, cabins were built. The WPA groups developed the fair grounds, the Auburn Ski Club at Cisco and built various retaining walls in and around Auburn. These can still be seen today.

AUBURN'S LINCOLN WAY (six views)

Courtesy Lee Photography

Lincoln Way with Old Auburn Post Office (left) and restored Firehouse (beyond)

Lincoln Way - 1920

Courtesy Lee Photography

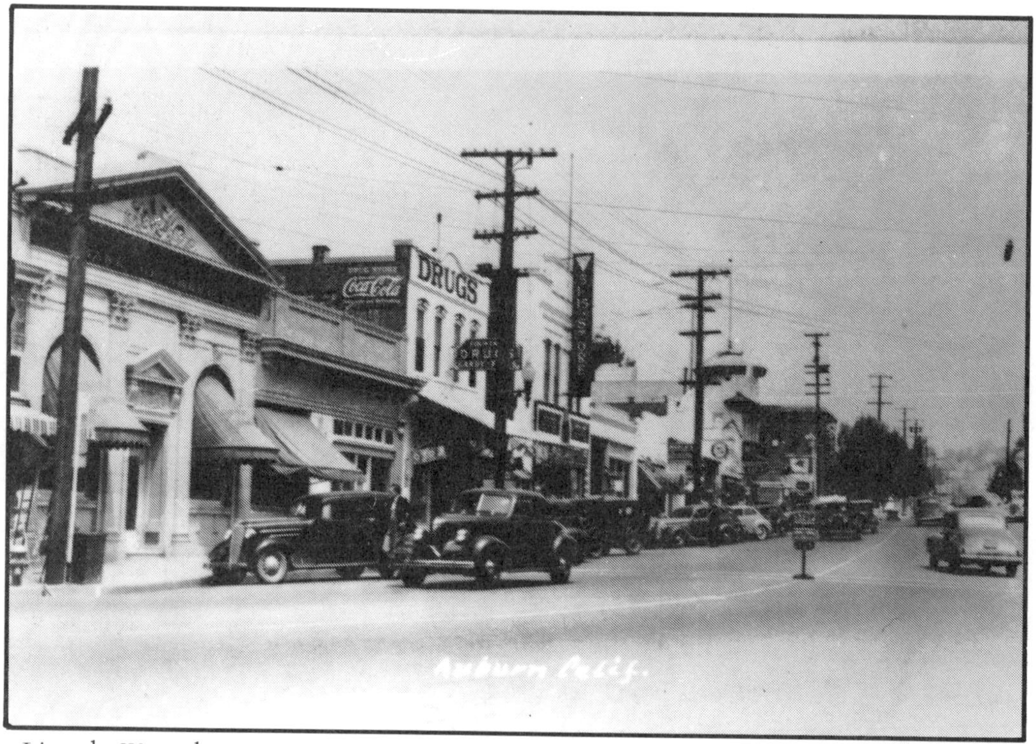

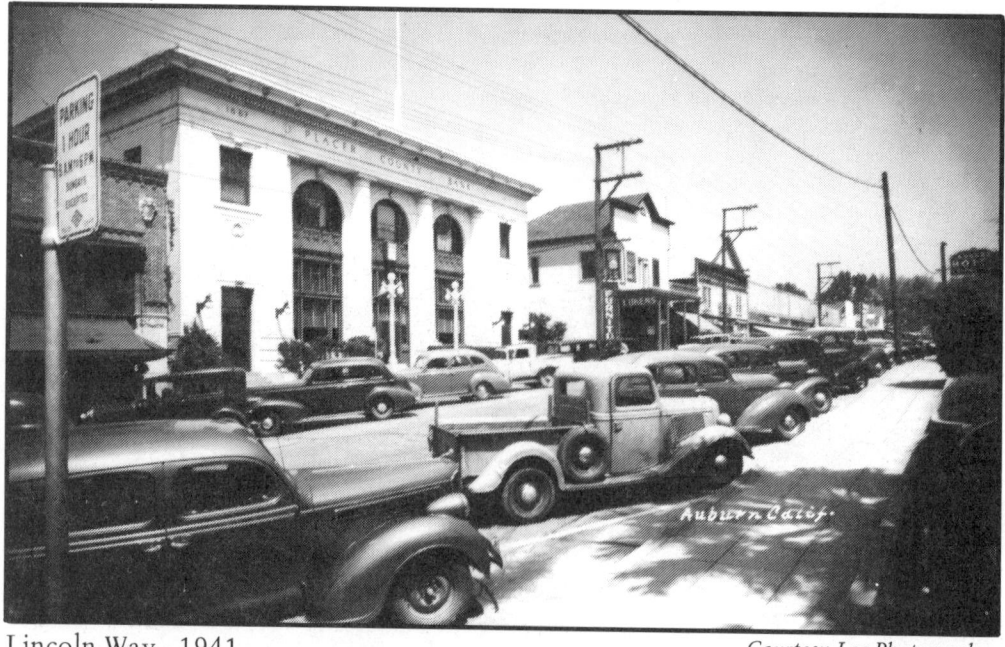

Lincoln Way - late 1930s *Courtesy Lee Photography*

Lincoln Way - 1941 *Courtesy Lee Photography*
Placer County Bank (left) and Lukens Hardware (beyond)
Auburn Hotel (right)

Courtesy Lee Photography

Lincoln Way (looking East) - 1930s or 1940s
Freeman Hotel (right) & Auburn Lumber Company (left)

Courtesy Lee Photography

Lincoln Way at the Freeman Hotel - 1941

These were years of construction for Auburn. In addition to the fair grounds, including erecting the building currently housing the Placer County Museum, there were the improvements to the Placer Junior College. Work began on the dam. With the dam came a labor contract and a cooperative effort developed with the A. F. of L. Labor disputes were rare in Auburn, however, there was an attempted takeover by the C. I. O. The Auburn Journal headlines on May 12, 1938 read, "CIO LEADERS INVADE CITY."

By the end of the 1930s, Auburn had developed a community resuscitation unit at the Freeman Hotel; a drive was underway to establish the Sisters of Mercy's Motherhouse on the Teagarden Tract and night football came to Auburn. This was also the year the Weber tragedy was revived. The Weber case was fictionalized and broadcast on Friday, November 18, 1938, on the "Crime Doesn't Pay Hour."[145] Auburn's citizens felt the producers of the radio show were too free with the facts of the case. This was also the time in history that the world was moving closer and closer to World War II.

World War II

> October 17, 1940 "...637 men register in Auburn."
> *Auburn Journal*

> November 23, 1940 "...nation's first peace-time conscription."
> *Auburn Journal*

> December 7, 1940 "...aliens have had three months in which to register."
> *The Placer Herald*

By 1940, America's involvement in the growing world conflict was inevitable. Auburn would experience some of the saddest moments in its history.

> "JACL (Japanese American Citizens League) PLEDGES LOYALTY IN CONFLICT, JACLs pleaded for tolerance and fair play through the duration of the conflict."
> *Auburn Journal, Monday, December 8, 1941*

Executive Order of the President, No. 9102, establishing the War Relocation Authority, began March 18, 1942. It ended June 30, 1946. This was a time of uncertainty and fear. Long smoldering racism gave way to expression. Auburn was in turmoil and at times divided. Established families were displaced and property lost. Even those Japanese-Americans in uniform were in jeopardy.

In June of 1943 a Japanese-American native of a near-by town, who had enlisted while at the Tule Lake Relocation Center, was on his way through Placer County. He was in a United States military uniform and stopped at Loomis. He was picked up by law enforcement officers, taken to Auburn and placed on a bus for his Oregon destination.

> "The Men's Club of Loomis had recently passed a resolution opposing the appearance of persons of Japanese descent in Loomis for the duration."[146]

This was also a time for expression of friendship. Japanese families were given short notice to leave their homes and farms. One such family had non-Japanese friends who came to their farm and cared for it during their absence.[147]

These were also the years of Victory Gardens, war bonds, rationing and the establishment of an Army hospital in Auburn.

The DeWitt Army General Hospital

If the Japanese internment and loss of young lives in the war were among Auburn's saddest moments, then among its proudest had to be the establishment of DeWitt Army General Hospital.

> "Aim at something substantial, don't fight over any particular location. Get the hospital first."

W. B. Shepard, then proprietor of The Placer Herald, wrote these words at the close of his editorial of September 5, 1942, as a challenge to the community to bring a "government hospital, a convalescent unit, into Auburn." Mr. Shepard continued,

> "...Auburn had no war activity, nothing to bring people here, and nothing to increase the interest in this phase of our war effort."[148]

Auburn's citizens responded to Shepard's challenge. Community leaders contacted Congressman Harry L. Englebright. Then they contacted the U. S. Army Surgeon General and finally the U. S. Army District Engineer. A representative of the District Engineer's Office from Sacramento came to Auburn. He toured the several possible sites with a local citizens group. The group chose a 186 acre site, four miles northwest of Auburn. In March of 1943, the United States Congress appropriated the necessary funds. DeWitt Army General Hospital was on its way to becoming a reality. The name of the hospital became

effective September 1, 1943, by government order — a tribute to Brigadier General Calvin DeWitt.

General DeWitt (1840-1909) served first in the Civil War. Later, after completing medical school, he reentered the army. He served for the remainder of his military career in a medical capacity. DeWitt took part in various Indian campaigns in Arizona and Northern California. Later, he served in the Spanish American War. By the 1900s, General DeWitt was a professor of Military Medicine at the Army Medical School and its president in 1902.

Although the first patient was admitted to DeWitt Army General Hospital on February 18, 1944, the official opening day was February 27, 1944. This was a day of excitement for the community. Speeches were made and the flag raised. Auburn's goal was realized and Shepard's challenge met.

The hospital was in continuous operation until December 31, 1945. During that time, the relationship between the hospital population and Auburn was, for the most part, a positive one.[149] Newspaper accounts reported community involvement with the hospital; both in direct volunteer work and in supplying such items as books, pianos and recreation equipment.

Not all relationships were positive. The following gives a hint of the reaction of a part of the community toward the Niseis (second generation Japanese).

> "Due to the fact that there was the Nisei problem which existed in this area (Auburn), there were quite a number of Nisei patients who did not take advantage of pass privileges because of the attitudes of various civilians in nearby communities."[150]

The Army included Nisei patients in local church activities and they had "badly crippled Nisei patients" make appearances in the community. Still,

> "...some merchants in the nearby town of Auburn continued to advertise the fact that Niseis were unwelcome, though this type of merchant was in the minority..."[151]

DeWitt Army General Hospital provided two newly developed services. On March 15, 1945, the hospital was selected as one of three speech centers for organic aphasiacs in the United States. While seven months before, August 23, 1944, the Army had established a Reconditioning Center at "Camp Flint."

> "The aim or purpose of this Reconditioning Center is to strengthen men who have had serious injuries, or have had major operations, until they are in shape to go back to duty, but, if that is impossible because of the nature of the injury, the man is discharged into civil life."[152]

The Center began with fifty patients. By January 18, 1945, the population had increased to approximately one hundred men at any one time.

By June 1945, two hundred German prisoners of war arrived and were housed at "Camp Flint." They assisted at the hospital in engineering, supply, laundry and food service until they left the camp in the early part of 1946. This was the end of "Camp Flint" (now the location of the Auburn fairgrounds). The buildings, other than two or three, were sold to local farmers for farm labor housing.[153] "Camp Flint" was vacated by the Army in early 1946. They didn't complete the release of the property back to the community until May and Auburn missed having a fair that year.

DeWitt Army General Hospital was discontinued December 31, 1945. The Army spent the next few months moving. Anyone who has moved, and had the lingering feeling they forgot something important, can sympathize with whoever "left the corpse in the hospital refrigerator unit," as reported in the Auburn Journal on June 24, 1946.

"WHY" Designed Sculptured and cast by Dr. Kenneth Fox. Dedicated to ALL the Fighting Men of the United States of America past-present-future

The Road Back

The road back was difficult for everyone after World War II. The Japanese surrender, aboard the battleship "Missouri" on September 2, 1945, did not change the attitude of some in the Auburn community toward persons of Japanese ancestry. However, Auburn was not alone in this negative attitude.

> "In much of rural California, however, particularly in the interior valleys from Imperial County on the Mexican border to Placer County, north and east of Sacramento, local feeling against the returnees was virulent; there was sporadic lawlessness, often abetted by law enforcement officials...In Placer County, for example, a mass meeting was called by a deputy sheriff, who was also commander of the local Veterans of Foreign Wars Post, to protest the return of the evacuated people and circulate a boycott pledge. Some in that county went further. The first Japanese to return to Placer County was the Doi family, who had sons in the armed forces."[154]

Sumio Doi, a graduate of Placer Union High School, was 26 years of age when he returned to his ranch near Auburn in early January, 1945. He had spent three years at a "relocation center" in Amache, Colorado. One of his first acts upon returning to his community was to register with the Placer County Selective Service Board. While Doi was putting his ranch and life in order, the Placer County Citizens Anti-Japanese League was being formed. There was a strong direction toward boycotting the returning people of Japanese ancestry. But, the League warned against violence toward these returnees for fear of reprisals against Americans still held as prisoners of war by the Japanese.

The keynote speaker at one of the early meetings of the Placer County Citizens Anti-Japanese League answered the question of,

> "...what would I like to see done with them (returnees)? Just this: I would like to see everyone of them go back to Japan and stay there and enjoy themselves in their own way and leave us to enjoy ourselves without them. If this is really a free country we should be free from interference from Japs or any other foreign nationals..."[155]

In the early morning hours of January 18 and 19, 1945, the Doi home, and packing sheds, were dynamited and burned. This was the greeting to this returning Japanese-American with two brothers serving in the United States Army. There were persons arrested and charged with these acts of violence. The Placer County Citizens Anti-Japanese League changed its name to the California Preservation Association and stated they were, "...opposed to acts of violence."[156] By July 26,

1945, those being tried for these acts were acquitted or found not guilty.

Life in Auburn, by the 1940s, had reached a level of complexity the founders never imagined. But then, those early arrivers had never really planned to create a town, only their fortunes. Auburn had seen a hundred years of development, growth and change. With the end of World War II, the town moved into a new era of prosperity. Progress had its price as landmarks of the past began to disappear.

THE COURT HOUSE - AUBURN

THEN
(before 1913)

NOW (1986)

Lower Auburn - circa 1900

Courtesy Lee Photography

7

Auburn — The Next Fifty Years

The Price Of Progress

The gathering of a few miners in Auburn's gulches and ravines gave way to an irregularly arranged but picturesque town. Its streets, once the trails to surrounding mines, are now thoroughfares to surrounding cities. The automobile replaced the stagecoach and train. Auburn, in the late 1940s, moved away from the sorrow of World War II and into an era of prosperity and growth. This progress had its price as reminders of the past began disappearing.

Former Lieutenant Governor Jacob H. Neff's home had fallen victim to progress when in March, 1937, "Agard Street was cut through from the high school to Lincoln Way."[157] The expansion of Highway 40 (now I80) gave Auburn new traffic problems. However, it allowed easier access to Sacramento and provided a true "gateway" to the foothills. With this expansion Auburn lost a long-time newspaper building and The Pioneer Memorial Fountain.

During the mid-1940s, The Placer Herald Building was condemned and by 1949 there had been an unsuccessful attempt to remove the fountain. In 1913 the Women's Improvement Club of Auburn had donated the fountain as a tribute to the town's pioneers.[158] They placed it in Lower Auburn's Plaza area. By November 10, 1950, the fountain was torn down to make room for the expanding highway. This plaque with the inscription:

> TO THE MEMORY OF PLACER CO. PIONEERS
> LEST WE FORGET
> 1848   1913

can be seen in Lower Auburn (Old Town) across from the statue of Claude Chana.

How To Use DeWitt Army General Hospital

By early 1946 Auburn citizens were divided over how to make use of the now vacant Army hospital. The Chamber of Commerce had gone on record as opposing the establishment of either a mental or tubercular institution at the DeWitt site.[159] By April of that year a group formed. It claimed Auburn would "acquire a stigma" and would be a less than desirable "home community."[160] The former DeWitt Army General Hospital was destined to become DeWitt State Hospital.

The State of California purchased the property and buildings on June 25, 1946. The first patient arrived on October 10, 1946. DeWitt was originally intended only as a transfer facility to relieve overcrowding in other similar California institutions. By 1950, the California State Legislature appointed DeWitt State Hospital a "permanent mental hospital and authorized commitments of mentally ill patients."[161] This hospital continued in Auburn until its closure by the State of California in the early 1970s. It had at one time "...the largest permanent payroll in the Auburn area."[162]

Auburn In The 1950s & 1960s

Auburn has always been a politically cognizant town. During the 1950s it was visited by Richard Nixon and James Roosevelt. In March, 1950, Governor Earl Warren joined the Lions for dinner at the Freeman Hotel.[163] In March of 1950 the registered voters in Auburn were shown as follows: Democrats 1,371 and Republicans 1,272.

Old Well At The Plaza

Courtesy State Historical Resources Commission

With the removal of the race barrier to citizenship (Oriental Exclusion Act, 1926), 1950 was also the year that about one thousand Japanese in Placer County became United States citizens.[164] These were also the years of strenuous effort by the federal government to integrate Native Americans, over their protests, into the larger society. As a part of this overall plan, President Truman on May 24, 1950, ordered payment to all Native Americans. These funds came from the old treaty rights trust funds. By July, 1950, Auburn's Indians "received a $150 per capita payment."[165]

In 1962 Harry J. Busselen, Jr., conducted a study of the Auburn Rancheria. His purpose was to understand the social and economic effects of the federal government's termination of California's Rancherias. The Auburn Rancheria land had been purchased by the federal government for the local Native Americans in 1910. Fifty-two years later the United States Government, through the Bureau of Indian Affairs, ended its trusteeship over the land. It was then turned over to the Native American residents with uninsurable land titles. These residents, with a mean income of less than two thousand dollars a year and with three or more children per family, were faced with water and sewer problems and accompanying state and local requirements. Busselen cites from the Committee on California Indians, Progress Report, 1954 Legislature, and writes the following,

> "The social integration of the Indians into the American community has been very limited. Only during the last twenty-five years or so have they been accepted as full citizens within the State of California. Within the County of Placer and the City of Auburn their acceptance has been limited, for although the schools in the Auburn area have been open to them since 1935, their acceptance in the schools has been minimal."[166]

Lincoln Way - 1950s

Courtesy Lee Photography

In 1959 another Auburn landmark, the Orleans Hotel, disappeared in the path of progress. Early that year the entire Orleans Block was in the process of being sold to Shell Oil Company. A group of Auburn citizens came forward in an attempt to save this historic building. The Auburn Journal of February 12, 1959, published a request from this citizens group for money pledges to help save the Orleans. A week later, the Chamber of Commerce made the following statement,

> "Public support of a drive to raise funds for the project was disappointing."
>
> *Auburn Journal, February 19, 1959*

The Orleans Hotel, built of native stone in the 1850s and survivor of several Lower Auburn fires was demolished in 1959.

By the summer of 1959, Auburn had another first. It had completed the final stages for annexing approximately one hundred and eighty-five acres. About one hundred and thirty-five of these acres were to the south of Auburn and about fifty acres were to the north.[167]

Auburn developed a General Plan in 1964 and anticipated that the community would triple its population in the next thirty years.[168] In the first fifty years of the twentieth century Auburn had more than doubled its population. The census of 1900 showed 2,050 people compared to 4,653 in 1950. The intervening years, however, had seen a drop in population from 2,376 in 1910 to 2,289 in 1920. Then a steady increase with 2,661 in 1930. By 1940, Auburn boasted a population of 4,013. The city's population was estimated in this plan to reach 15,000 by 1990.[169] The Auburn General Plan of 1964 listed the community's goals: continuing as the Placer County seat, as the "gateway" to Sierra recreation, as a major trading center for the County and travelers through the county and as a "desirable place to live and work."[170] Therefore, Auburn eagerly welcomed President Johnson's signature on the Auburn Dam Project in 1965.

Plans were developing for a new hospital (Auburn Faith Community Hospital) in the 1960s and the completed I80 highway was dedicated in October, 1964. Building was "booming in Auburn" during these years. Building permits increased from 424 in 1951 to 928 in 1963.[171] Then Auburn had another fire. This time the Auburn Fruit Exchange Building, on Nevada Street, burned. Although there were some one hundred people employed, there were no deaths. There was, however, extensive property damage.[172]

The End Of An Era

T. H. Watkins traveled by train through Auburn in the late 1960s or early 1970s. He stopped here briefly and witnessed and then wrote about the end of another Auburn landmark — the Freeman Hotel.[173] This hotel was built as West's in 1866 fronting on what was then Railroad Avenue (now Lincoln Way) across from the train depot. The hotel burned and was rebuilt in 1868. It was later called the Borland and was bought by Freeman in the early 1880s. The third story annex was added in the late 1890s. In later years this hotel became the "headquarters for Southern Pacific engineers in the Rocklin to Colfax cut off construction job that lasted until 1912."[174] The hotel burned again. It was rebuilt and opened the night of President Taft's election, November 4, 1908.[175] The hotel's location, directly across the street from the train depot, made it an ideal stopping place for travelers through Auburn. It was also the scene of many community events over the years. The old "railroad hotel" was torn down with community regret and replaced by a shopping center.

The Future

On February 5, 1979, the Auburn City Council adopted The Auburn Area General Plan. It amended the first Auburn General Plan of 1964. This 1979 Plan is the official statement and guide for the development of the City of Auburn until 1995. During the drafting of this second plan, Charles Brau researched "existing attitudes among the residents of the Auburn area concerning population growth and growth limitations measure." He reached the following conclusion:

> "A majority of residents of Auburn do not want the Auburn area to grow at a rate consistent with that rate planned for in the Draft Auburn Area General Plan. A majority of Auburn residents feel that Auburn could use a growth limitation and management system."[176]

Orleans Hotel, Auburn

Courtesy California State Library

Auburn — 1986

Auburn's development was similar to other western mining camps of the 1850s, however, it did not fall victim to abandonment when the gold ran out. The town's location, the tenacity of its citizens, the warm summers amd mild winters ensured its survival.

Auburn of 1986 continues a blend of rugged past and sophisticated new. The now vacant Placer County Court House waits patiently for restoration and the Auburn Dam Project may yet become a reality. Old Auburn (Lower Auburn) continues to attract visitors as it did in years past; but, they come now to see history, not create it.

It is possible to travel on a single street, Lincoln Way, from beginning to end and see much of the old and new that is Auburn today. By traveling northeast from Sacramento on I80 and taking the Maple Street "turnoff" the visitor is suddenly thrust into Auburn's past. This street was once called Main Street. The huge statue of Chana can be seen on the right and the site of the Orleans Hotel to the left. The restored firehouse (complete with bell), the old post office and Chinese houses can still be seen. Concerned members of the community have placed plaques at several historical sites, such as the Placer County Bank Building and G. Willment's Store, lest these be lost to time. Only the brick wall of the American Hotel remains standing at the side of the Shanghai Restaurant. The Placer Herald sign can be seen in Lower Auburn, a reminder of the past. A past which once saw a City Hall and Opera House in Old Auburn.

Traveling up Lincoln Way (once Broad Street) the Methodist Church can be seen just beyond the now silent Court House. Continuing on Lincoln Way, the Auburn School Building is on the right and the Catholic Church on the left. Then on to what was once called Central Square. Just beyond is the site of Auburn's Opera House. Passing the just vacated Post Office we are now in Auburn's "downtown" area with such businesses as Seva Books in Gold Country Mall and Lee Photography on the right. A left turn at Elm Street will take the visitor past what was once the Placer County Hospital (now Auburn Town Center) and on to the old Auburn Cemetery and Nevada Street. However, continuing on Lincoln Way (once Railroad Avenue) we pass the site of the Freeman Hotel, Auburn Depot and Martin Park. Trains no longer stop in Auburn but one can travel to Colfax and catch the 2:24 p.m. daily Amtrack for points east. Lincoln Way continues on north past Foresthill Avenue which was once a busy stagecoach route. Then on to the new Foresthill Road and past a nearly new bustling shopping center. Our travels on Lincoln Way end a few miles beyond this center.

"Sweet Auburn! lovliest village of the plain;
Where health and plenty cheared the labouring swain,
Where smiling spring its earliest visit paid,
And parting summer's lingering blooms delayed:..."
    The Deserted Village by Oliver Goldsmith (1728-1774)

Epilogue

I hope you have enjoyed this brief journey through Auburn's past, present and future. Further growth and development seems to have been Auburn's destiny from the beginning. The community continues to struggle with progress while still maintaining the small town spirit. Hopefully progress can coexist with preservation of Auburn's rich heritage. Auburn has always coped with diversity and adversity. Through it all this town has maintained its integrity to become one of the most interesting foothill communities in Northern California.

CHANGE

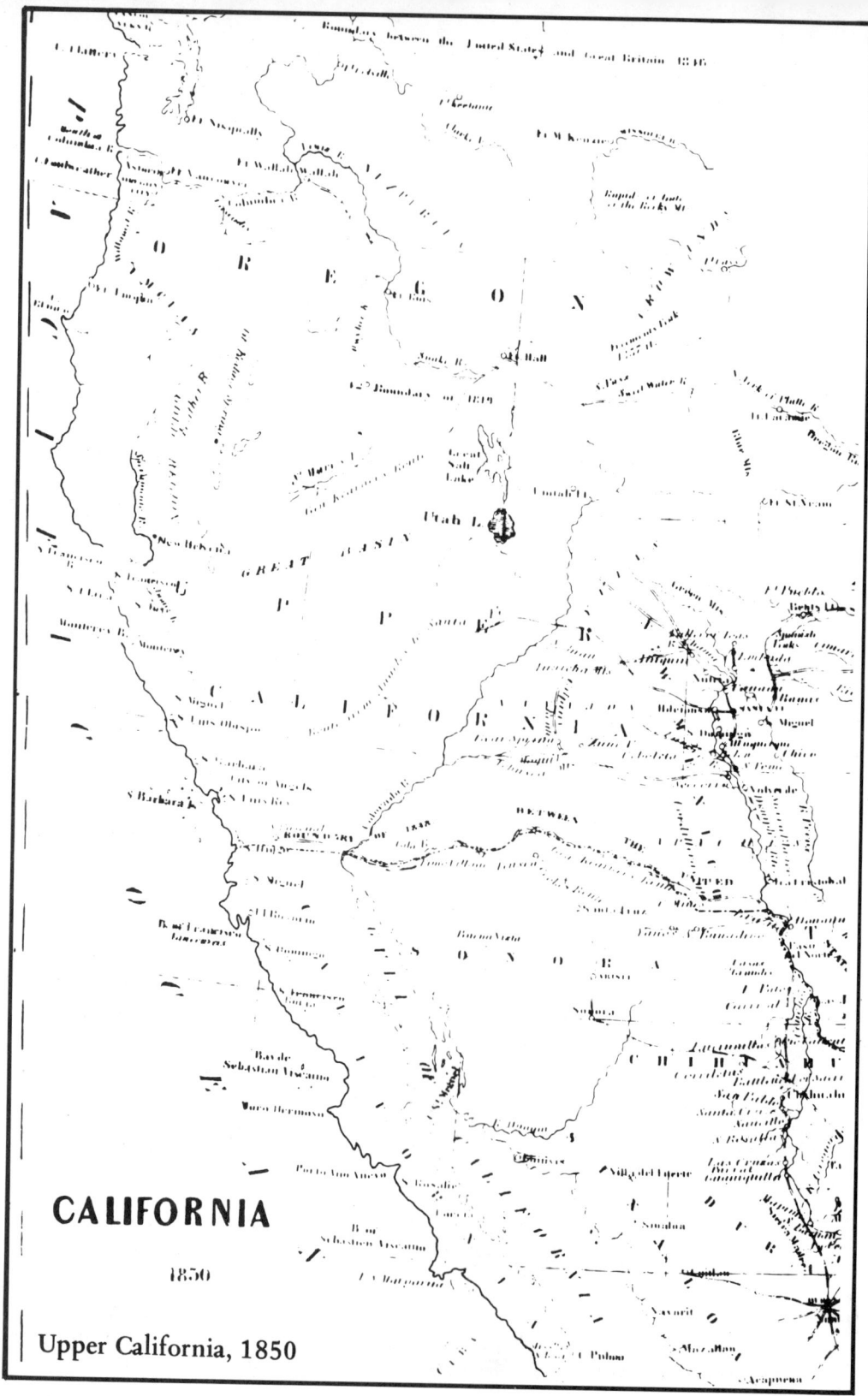

Auburn won't appear on a California map until 1851.

Courtesy Northern Map Company

Notes

Chapter 1

1. Walsh, Henry L., *Hallowed Were The Gold Dust Trails,* University of Santa Clara Press, 1946.
2. Cleland, Robert Glass, *From Wilderness To Empire, A History Of California,* Alfred A. Knopf, New York, 1959.
3. Cutter, Donald D., Translator & Editor, *The Diary of Ensign Gabriel Moraga's Expedition of Discovery in the Sacramento Valley, 1808,* Glen Dawson Publisher, 1957.

    Gabriel Moraga, son of Jose Joaquin Moraga, a second-generation explorer was also known to have a record number of confrontations with Indians in California. Gabriel Moraga's diary was found in the archives of the Santa Barbara Mission.
4. Cleland, *op. cit.*
5. Schlesinger, Jr., Arthur M., Editor, *The Almanac of American History,* G. P. Putnam's Sons, New York, 1983.
6. Tyler, Sgt. Daniel, *A Concise History of the Mormon Battalion in the Mexican War, 1846-1848,* The Rio Grande Press, Inc., New Mexico, first published 1881, second printing 1969.

    There is a George Wilson listed as a Private in Company E of the Mormon Battalion.
7. Bennett, William P., *The First Baby In Camp,* The Rancher Publishing Co., Salt Lake City, Utah, 1893.
8. Angel, Myron, *History of Placer County,* Thompson & West, Historic Record Co., Oakland, 1882.
9. Steele, R. J., *Directory of the County of Placer, For The Year 1861,* San Francisco, 1861.
10. Clark, Francis, "Stevenson's Regiment in California," *The New York Volunteers In California,* The Rio Grande Press, Inc., New Mexico, first published 1882, first printing 1970.
11. Reinhardt, Richard, "The Tammany Pioneers," *A Sense of History,* American Heritage, Houghton Mifflin Co., Boston, 1985.
12. Clark, *op. cit.*
13. Angel, *op. cit.*

    E. D. Shirland is also listed on April 15, 1882, as a New York Volunteer survivor living in Auburn, Placer County in Clark's "Stevenson's Regiment in California."

14. Monaghan, Jay, *Chile, Peru And The California Gold Rush of 1849*, University of California Press, 1973.

    California Historical Landmarks, published by the California Department of Parks & Recreation, 1979, has recorded the following in reference to El Dorado County's Historical Landmark No. 569 – Mormon Island:

    "Early in March 1848, W. Sidney, S. Willis and Wilford Hudson, members of the Mormon Battalion, set out from Sutter's Fort to hunt deer. Stopping on the south fork of the American River, they found gold. They told their story on returning to the fort, and soon about 150 Mormons and other miners flocked to the site, which was named Mormon Island. This was the first major gold strike in California after James W. Marshall's discovery at Coloma..."

    California Historical Landmarks also lists No. 530 – Gold Discovery Site (El Dorado County). The monument there marks the actual site of Marshall's discovery on January 24, 1848. The Society of California Pioneers "definitely located and marked the site in 1924..."
15. *Ibid.*
16. Angel, *op. cit.*
17. Steele, *op. cit.*
18. Lardner, W. B. and M. J. Brock, *History of Placer And Nevada Counties, California,* Historic Record Company, Los Angeles, 1924.
19. Placer Weekly Argus, *Placer County Business & Official Directory, 1875,* Auburn, California, 1875.
20. Carter, John D., "George Kenyon Fitch, Pioneer California Journalist," *California Historical Society Quarterly,* Volume 20, 1941.
21. Delavan, James, *Notes On California And The Placer, How To Get There, And What To Do Afterwards* first published in 1850, Biobook, Oakland, California, 1956.
22. Frost, John, *History of The State of California,* Derby & Miller, Auburn, New York, 1850.
23. Placer County Republican, December 17, 1903.

    This article places Mrs. Crandall in Placer County in December, 1851; however, in C. W. Haskins' *The Argonauts of California* there is a listing of an H. J. Crandall on the Bark "Rhodes," from Providence, November, 1849.
24. Morgan, Sister Mary Evangelist, *Mercy, Generation To Generation,* Fearon Publishers, San Francisco, 1957.

    Sister Mary Evangelist was a native of Auburn, educated by the Sisters of Mercy at St. Joseph's Academy in Sacramento, entered the novitiate there in 1915 and her "profession...was witnessed by a large concourse" at St. Joseph's Academy in Sacramento. Auburn Journal, March 12, 1918.
25. Vassault, F., "A Story In Transition," *The Overland Monthly,* January, 1891, Volume 17, Number 93.
26. California Historical Society, "Stephen Hodge Mann, Stockton Pioneer (his correspondence 1848-1864)," Vol. 31, No. 3, San Francisco, September 1952.

27. Tyson, MD, James L., *Diary Of A Physician In California*, Biobooks, Oakland, California, first published in 1850, printed 1955.
28. Fairchild, M. D., "Reminiscences of a Forty-Niner," *California Historical Society Quarterly*, Volume 13, Number 1.

    Fairchild's date of naming Auburn coincides with Samuel W. Halladay's statement, "By virtue of my august authority as Alcalde, in August, 1849, I named our diggings Auburn. As such, the place is recorded on Butler's Map, 1851." In Gudde, Erwin G., *California Place Names*, University of California Press, 1949.
29. Vischer, Eduard, "Californischer Staats-Kalender" (A Trip To The Mining Regions In The Spring Of 1859), *California Historical Society Quarterly*, Volume 2, 1932.

Chapter 2

30. Schlesinger, *op. cit.*
31. Cleland, Robert Glass, *A History of California: The American Period*, The MacMillan Company, 1923.

    "Celestial" is from The Celestial Empire, a popular name for the Chinese Empire, and refers to a native of China.
32. Angel, *op. cit.*
33. This information prepared and shared by Mr. and Mrs. Frank Delmar (Josephine Filcher Delmar). The Adams "Acorn" Press is 24 inches by 36 inches and has serial number 265.
34. Placer County, Auburn City Census, 1860.
35. Suit Number 2046 Jackson, Chesterfield vs. James Howard, March 10, 1865, Judgment Number 1345 page in Judgment Book D 134 page in Minute Book 487 (District Court 14th Judicial District).
36. Lapp, Rudolph M., *Blacks In Gold Rush California*, Yale University Press, 1977.
37. Lardner, *op. cit.*
38. Lapp, *op. cit.*
39. Lapp, *op. cit.*
40. Davis, Leonard M., *A Study of An Early California Mining Camp*, Thesis, 1953.
41. Lapp, *op. cit.*
42. Lapp, *op. cit.*
43. Wheat, Carl I., Editor, "California's Bantam Cock, The Journals of Charles E. DeLong, 1854-1863," *California Historical Society Quarterly*, Volume 9, 1930.
44. Placer County Republican, December 17, 1903.
45. Walsh, *op. cit.*
46. Auburn Journal, September 7, 1972.

47. This information and the writings by Irene A. Burns found in the Archives of the Placer County Office of Education.
48. The Placer Herald, December 23, 1871.
49. 1872 Ledger, Archives, Placer County Office of Education.
50. From the writings of Irene A. Burns found in the Archives of the Placer County Office of Education.
51. Darrah, Estelle, Stanford University, from the Minutes of November 7, 1895, Archives, Placer County Office of Education.
52. Minutes of 1896, Archives, Placer County Office of Education.
53. Graham, William, "An Analysis of the Origin and Development of the Placer County Hospital and the Emergence of Hospital Policy," Thesis, 1966.
54. Ibid.
55. Ibid.

Hannah Lloyd Neall's letter of January 8, 1864, from Auburn (on page 36) is recorded by Marie D. Dun in the *California Historical Society Quarterly*, Volume 31, Number 3, San Francisco, September, 1952.

Chapter 3

56. The Placer Herald, July 13 and 16, August 13, 1859.
    The dedication of the "Rattlesnake Dick" Memorial Stone is reported in the Auburn Journal of May 22, 1969. The dedication was preceded by a luncheon at the fairgrounds and was attended by 300 people. Of these, 200 were school children from Auburn Union and St. Joseph's Schools.
57. Winther, Oscar O., *Via Western Express & Stagecoach*, Stanford University Press, 1945.
58. Loomis, Noel M., *Wells Fargo, An Illustrated History*, Clarkson N. Potter, Inc., New York, 1968.
59. Beebe, Lucius, *The Central Pacific & The Southern Pacific Railroads*, Howell-North, Berkeley, 1963.
60. Angel, *op. cit.*
61. Angel, *op. cit.*
62. Fulton, Robert L., *Epic of The Overland*, Kovach, Los Angeles, 1954.
63. Ibid.
64. Ibid.
65. Tza-Kuei, Yen, "Chinese Workers And The First Transcontinental Railroad of The United States of America," Dissertation, St. John's University, New York, 1976.
66. Ibid.
67. Ibid.
68. Ibid.
69. Ibid.

70. *Ibid.*
71. *Ibid.* "Six Companies" is a common term for the Chinese Consolidated Benevolent Association. This association was founded in 1854 by Cantonese merchants. See Frank Viviano's article, "The Asianization of California (and vice versa)" in *Golden State Report,* August, 1986, for information concerning this association.
72. *Ibid.*
    California Historical Landmarks, published by the California Department of Parks and Recreation, 1979, has recorded Historical Landmark (Placer County) Number 780.4 — First Transcontinental Railroad, and states the following:
    "After an 11-month delay due to political opposition and lack of money, Central Pacific tracks reached Auburn May 13, 1865, and regular service began. Government loans became available when the railroad completed its first 40 miles, four miles east of here..."
73. Fulton, *op. cit.*
    There are several versions of Timothy Hopkins' natural father's death. Timothy was born Timothy W. Nolan in Augusta, Maine, the son of Catherine and Patrick Nolan. Oscar Lewis writes that Patrick Nolan "fell into the bay (San Francisco) and was drowned," while Estelle Latta writes "His (Tim's) father had died during the long overland journey to California in 1862," and, finally, Dallas E. Wood writes that Tim's "father lost his life by drowning soon after arrival in this state." All agree that Tim was legally adopted by Mrs. Hopkins in 1879.
74. Reinhardt, Richard, *Workin' On The Railroad,* American West Publishing Company, Palo Alto, California, 1970.
75. Wooster, Clarence M., "Railroading In California In The Seventies," *California Historical Society Quarterly,* Volume 18, 1939.
76. Placer County Republican, December 17, 1903.
77. The Placer Herald, September 3, 1870.
78. *Ibid.*

Chapter 4

79. Cleland, Robert Glass, *A History of California: The American Period,* The MacMillan Company, 1923.
80. *Ibid.*
81. Placer Weekly Argus, *Placer County Business & Official Directory, 1875,* Auburn, California, 1875.
82. Angel, *op. cit.*
83. May, Philip Ross, *Origins Of Hydraulic Mining In California,* The Holmes Book Company, Oakland, California, 1970.
84. *Ibid.*
85. Auburn Journal, July 4, 1929.

86. Cosby, Stanley W. and E. B. Watson and W. G. Harper, *Soil Survey of the Auburn Area, California,* U. S. Government Printing Office, 1928.
87. *Ibid.*
88. *Ibid.*
89. Angel, *op. cit.*
90. Filcher, Hon. J. A., "Looking Back," *The Placer Herald,* published between 1922-1923, loaned to the author by Mrs. Josephine Filcher Delmar.
91. Lardner, *op. cit.*
92. Placer Weekly Argus, January 11, 1884.
93. Placer Weekly Argus, April 16, 1884.
94. Angel, *op. cit.*
95. The Placer Herald, April 11, 1885.
96. Kitano, Harry H. L., *Japanese Americans The Evolution of a Subculture,* Prentice-Hall, Inc., New Jersey, 1969.
97. Wilson, Robert A. and Bill Hosokawa, *East To America A History of the Japanese In The United States,* Wm. Morrow & Co., New York, 1980.

    California Historical Landmarks, published by the California Department of Parks and Recreation, 1979, has recorded the following in reference to El Dorado County's Historical Landmark Number 815 — Wakamatsu Tea And Silk Farm Colony;

    "The agricultural settlement of pioneer Japanese immigrants who arrived at Gold Hill on June 8, 1869 - the only tea and silk farm established in California - had a promising outlook but failed tragically in less than two years. This was the initial Japanese-influenced agricultural attempt in California. Gold Hill and Gold Springs Roads, Gold Hill, El Dorado County."
98. Kitano, *op. cit.*

Chapter 5

99. *Memorial & Biographical History of Northern California, Illustrated,* The Lewis Publishing Company, Chicago, 1891.
100. Lardner, *op. cit.*

     The term "dedication" is used in published reports of the activities related to the "new" Placer County Court House in Auburn during the summer of 1894. John Trumbo, Auburn Journal, April 16, 1986, states; "The courthouse was dedicated July 4, 1894." The "historical landmark" near the courthouse, however, states:

     SITE OF FIRST PUBLIC
     HANGING AREA & GRAVEYARD – THIRD
     COURT HOUSE CORNERSTONE
     LAID July 4, 1894
     dedicated July 4, 1898

     There is discrepancy concerning the date the courthouse bell was bought.

It may have been 1854 or 1859, although, Trumbo in his article for the Auburn Journal, March 28, 1975, states that the three hundred pound bell is inscribed NAYLOR VICKERS & CO. 1859. The bell can be seen on the north side of the courthouse at the edge of the dome. It was apparently used in years past to call tardy lawyers and witnesses to court.

101. The Placer Herald, November 21, 1891.
102. Minute Book for the Placer County Teachers Institute of 1896, Archives, Placer County Office of Education.
103. Lardner, *op. cit.*
104. *Ibid.*
105. *Ibid.*
106. Auburn Journal, May 5, 1918. "Wobblies was the term used for the IWW members. The Wheatland Riot was a major event in the unrest of the migratory workers and a discussion of this can be found in *California Heartland,* "The Wheatland Riot," by Carey McWilliams, Capra Press, Santa Barbara, 1978.
107. *Auburn City Directory, 1899.* This directory contains a list of residents of Auburn, principal business firms, hotels, points of interest and other general information. It also contains an "authorized copy" of the Ordinances of the City of Auburn.
108. Graham, *op. cit.*
109. Auburn Journal, July 28, 1932. Accounts of Weber's arrest and trial can be found in the Placer County Republican between November 17, 1904, and February 22, 1905.
110. The Placer Herald, September 29, 1906.
111. Folsom State Prison Records.
112. The Placer Herald, September 29, 1906.
113. The Placer Herald, October 6, 1906.
114. *Ibid.*
115. Placer County Republican, July 27, 1905.
116. *Ibid.*
117. The Placer Herald, November 16, 1907.
118. The Placer Herald, September 14, 1911.

Chapter 6

119. Cleland, Robert Glass, *California In Our Time, 1900:1940,* Alfred A. Knopf, New York, 1947.
120. The Placer Herald, September 14, 1911.
121. The Placer Herald, May 9, 1914.
122. Lardner, *op. cit.*
123. Auburn Journal, January 5, 1918.
124. Auburn Journal, April 3, 1918.

125. Auburn Journal, January 8, 1918.
126. Graham, *op. cit.*
127. Auburn Journal, February 4, 1918.
128. Lardner, *op. cit.*
129. Auburn Journal, January 26, 1918. The "scare" concerned a special type of pollen in the wheat crop which destroyed the plant.
130. Auburn Journal, January 7, 1918.
131. Schlesinger, *op. cit.*
132. Auburn Journal & Placer County Republican, November 14, 1918.
133. Auburn Journal & Placer County Republican, January 2, 1919.
134. Auburn Journal & Placer County Republican, August 1, 1929.
135. Auburn Journal & Placer County Republican, August 2, 1929.
136. Auburn Journal, November 12, 1931.
137. Auburn Journal, January 21, 1932.
138. Auburn Journal, July 30, 1931.
139. Auburn Journal, February 18, 1932.
140. Auburn Journal, December 15 and 8, 1932.
141. Graham, *op. cit.*
142. Auburn Journal & Placer County Republican, January 6, 1938.
143. Auburn Journal, February 23, 1939.
144. Auburn Journal, July 14 and 28, 1938.
145. Auburn Journal, November 24, 1938.
146. Auburn Journal, June 17, 1943.
147. Nakae, Tomeo (Okui), *Recollections,* donated to the Auburn-Placer County Library, 1982.
148. The Placer Herald, September 5, 1942.
149. Army Service Forces, Ninth Service Command, DeWitt General Hospital, *Annual Report for the Calender Year, 1944.*
150. Army Service Forces, Ninth Service Command, DeWitt General Hospital, *Annual Report for the Calender Year, 1945.*
151. *Ibid.*
152. Auburn Journal, January 18, 1945.
153. Auburn Journal, February 28, 1946.
154. Daniels, Roger, *Concentration Camps: North America Japanese in the United States and Canada During World War II,* Krieger Publishing Company, Florida, 1981.
155. The Journal Republican, January 18, 1945.
156. The Journal Republican, January 25, 1945.

Chapter 7

157. Sacramento Union, March 7, 1937.
158. Davis, *op. cit.* and the Auburn Journal, November 16, 1950.

159. Auburn Journal, February 14, 1946.
160. Auburn Journal, April 11, 1946.
161. *Auburn Chamber of Commerce,* Auburn-Placer County Library.
162. Auburn Journal, July 16, 1964.
163. Auburn Journal, March 16, 1950.
164. Auburn Journal, August 17, 1950.
165. Auburn Journal, July 6, 1950.
166. Busselen, Jr., Harry J., *A Study of The Federal Termination of A California Rancheria and Its Effect Upon The Social And Economic Integration of The Indian Population Involved,* Thesis, 1962. Placer County Office of Education provided the following information concerning the October, 1985, enrollment of Native American children in Placer County schools: There were 92 males and 100 females enrolled in twelve different schools. There were a total of 52 children in the Auburn Union School District and 32 in the Placer Joint Union High School.
167. Sacramento Bee, August 6, 1959.
168. *Auburn General Plan,* Placer County, California, 1964.
169. *Ibid.*
170. *Ibid.*
171. Auburn Journal, January 9, 1964.
172. Auburn Journal, September 4, 1969.
173. Watkins, T. H., "Who Killed The Railroad Hotel In Auburn?", *Westways,* April, 1971, Volume 63, Part I.
174. Sacramento Bee, 1946.
175. Sacramento Bee, 1946.
176. Brau, Charles, *Population Growth In The Auburn Area,* Thesis, 1979.

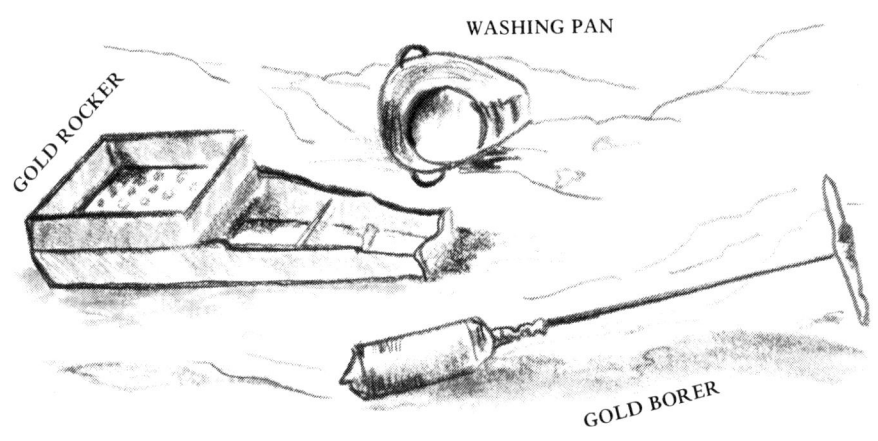

From Frost's History of California, 1850

Bibliography

Books

Angel, Myron, *History of Placer County,* Thompson & West, Historic Record Co., Oakland, California, 1882.

Atherton, Gertrude, *California An Intimate History,* Harper & Brothers Publisher, New York & London, 1914.

_____, *California An Intimate History, Revised,* Horace Liveright, New York, 1927.

Beebe, Lucius and Charles Clegg, *The Age of Steam,* Rinehart & Co., New York & Toronto, 1957.

Beebe, Lucius, *The Central Pacific & The Southern Pacific Railroads,* Howell-North Berkeley, California, 1963.

Bennett, William P., *The First Baby In Camp,* The Rancher Publishing Co., Salt Lake City, Utah, 1893.

Best, Gerald M., *Iron Horses To Promontory,* Golden West Books, 1969.

Brau, Charles, *Population Growth In The Auburn Area,* Thesis, California State University, Sacramento, California, 1979.

Busselen, Jr., Harry J., *A Study of The Federal Termination of A California Rancheria And Its Effect Upon The Social And Economic Integration of The Indian Population Involved,* Thesis, California State University, Sacramento, California, 1962.

Caughey, John Walton, *Gold Is The Cornerstone,* University of California Press, Berkeley and Los Angeles, California, 1948.

Clark, Francis, *The New York Volunteers In California,* "Stevenson's Regiment In California," The Rio Grande Press, Inc., New Mexico, first published 1896, printed 1970.

Cleland, Robert Glass, *A History of California: The American Period,* The Macmillan Co., New York, 1923.

_____, *California In Our Time, 1900-1940,* Alfred A. Knopf, New York, 1947.

_____, *From Wilderness To Empire,* Alfred A. Knopf, New York, 1959.

Cooper, Frederic Taber, *Rider's California, A Guide-Book For Travelers,* The Macmillan Co., New York & London, 1925.

Cosby, Stanley W. and E. B. Watson and W. G. Harper, *Soil Survey of The Auburn Area, California,* U. S. Government Printing Office, 1928.

Cutter, Donald D., Translator and Editor, *The Diary of Ensign Gabriel Moraga's Expedition of Discovery In The Sacramento Valley, 1808,* Glen Dawson Publisher, 1957.

Daniels, Roger, *Concentration Camps: North America Japanese In The United States And Canada During World War II,* Krieger Publishing Co., Florida, 1981.

Davis, Leonard M., *A Study of An Early California Mining Camp,* Thesis, California State University, Sacramento, California, 1953.

Delavan, James, *Notes On California And The Placers, How To Get There, And What To Do Afterwards,* Biobooks, Oakland, California, first published in 1850, printed in 1956.

Forbes, Jack D., *Native Americans of California And Nevada,* Naturegraph Publishers, Healdsburg, California, 1969.

Frost, John, *History of The State of California,* Derby & Miller, Auburn, New York, 1850.

Fulton, Robert Lardin, *Epic of The Overland,* A. M. Robertson, San Francisco, California, 1924.

Furnas, J. C., *The Americans, A Social History of The United States, 1587-1914,* G. P. Putnam's Sons, New York, 1969.

Gardiner, Howard C., *In Pursuit of The Golden Dream, Reminiscences of San Francisco And The Northern & Southern Mines, 1849-1857,* Western Hemisphere, Inc., Stoughton, Mass., 1970.

Graham, William, *An Analysis of The Origin And Development of The Placer County Hospital And The Emergence of Hospital Policy,* Thesis, California State University, Sacramento, California, 1966.

Grun, Bernard, *The Timetables of History,* Simon & Schuster, New York, 1978.

Haslam, Gerald W. and James D. Houston, Editors, *California Heartland, Writing From The Great Central Valley,* Capra Press, Santa Barbara, California, 1978.

Hawthorne, Hildegarde, *Romantic Cities of California,* Illustrated by E. H. Suydam, Appleton-Century-Crofts, Inc., New York and London, 1939.

Hoover, Mildred B., Hero E. Rensch and Ethel G. Rensch, *Historic Spots In California, Combined 3 Volumnes In 1,* Stanford University Press, Stanford, California, 1948.

——————————, *Historic Spots In California, 3rd Edition,* Stanford University Press, Stanford, California, 1966.

Jackson, Helen Hunt, *A Century of Dishonor,* Harper Torchbooks, The University Library, Harper & Row Publishers, New York, Evanston & London, 1881.

Jackson, Joseph Henry, *Anybody's Gold, The Story of California's Mining Towns,* Illustrated by E. H. Suydam, D. Appleton-Century Co., New York & London, 1941.

Johnson, Paul C., *Sierra Album,* Doubleday & Co., Garden City, New York, 1971.

Kelly, William, Esq., *A Stroll Through The Diggins of California,* Biobooks, Oakland, California, 1950.

Kitano, Harry H. L., *Japanese Americans The Evolution of A Subculture,* Prentice-Hall, Inc., New Jersey, 1969.

Kraus, George, *High Road To Promontory,* American West Publishing Co., California, 1969.

Lapp, Rudolph M., *Blacks In Gold Rush California,* Yale University Press, New Haven, Conn., and London, 1977.

Lardner, W. B. and M. J. Brock, *History of Placer And Nevada Counties, California,* Historic Record Company, Los Angeles, California, 1924.

Latta, Estelle, *Controversial Mark Hopkins,* Greenberg Publisher, New York, 1953.

Lewis, Oscar, *The Big Four,* Alfred A. Knopf, New York and London, 1938.

Loomis, Noel M., *Wells Fargo, An Illustrated History,* Clarkson N. Potter, Inc., New York, 1968.

Lynch, James, *The New York Volunteers In California,* "With Stevenson To California," The Rio Grande Press, Inc., New Mexico, first published 1882, printed in 1970.

Markham, Edwin, *Songs & Stories,* Powell Publishing Co., San Francisco, Los Angeles and Chicago, 1931.

May, Philip Ross, *Origins Of Hydraulic Mining In California,* The Holmes Book Company, Oakland, California, 1970.

Masri, Allan, *The Golden Hills of California, Volume II,* Western Tanager Press, Santa Cruz, California, 1983.

Monaghan, Jay, *Australians And The Gold Rush, California And Down Under 1849-1854,* University of California Press, Berkeley, California, 1966.

_____, *Chile, Peru And The California Gold Rush of 1849,* University of California Press, Berkeley, California, 1973.

Morgan, Neil, *The Pacific States,* Time-Life Books, Time, Inc., New York, 1967.

Morgan, Sister Mary Evangelist, *Mercy, Generation To Generation,* Fearon Publishers, San Francisco, California, First Edition, 1957.

Morris, Richard B., *Encyclopedia of American History,* Harper & Row, Publishers, New York, 1953.

Nakae, Tomeo (Okui), *Recollections,* Donated To The Auburn-Placer County Library, 1982.

Pearsall, Robert and Ursula S. Erickson, Editors, *The Californians: Writings of Their Past And Present, Volumes I and II,* Hesperian House, San Francisco, California, 1961.

Reinhardt, Richard, *A Sense of History,* "The Tammany Pioneers," American Heritage, Houghton Mifflin Co., Boston, Mass., 1985.

_____, Editor, *Workin' On The Railroad,* American West Publishing Co., Palo Alto, California, 1970.

Ross, Nancy Wilson, *Westward The Women,* Alfred A. Knopf, New York, 1944.

Schlesinger, Jr., Arthur M., *The Almanac of American History,* G. P. Putnam's Sons, New York, 1983.

Steele, R. J., *Directory of The County of Placer, For The Year 1861,* San Francisco, California, 1861.

Tza-Kuei, Yen, *Chinese Workers And The First Transcontinental Railroad of The United States of America,* Dissertation, St. John's University, New York, 1976.

Tyler, Sergeant Daniel, *A Concise History of The Mormon Battalion In The Mexican War, 1846-1847,* The Rio Grande Press, Inc., New Mexico, first published in 1881, second printing in 1969.

Tyson, MD, James L., *Diary of A Physician In California,* Biobooks, Oakland, California, first published in 1850, printed in 1955.

Urdang, Laurence, Editor, *The Timetables of American History,* Simon & Schuster, New York, 1980.

Walsh, Henry L., *Hallowed Were The Gold Dust Trails, The Story of The Pioneer Priests of Northern California,* University of Santa Clara Press, Santa Clara, California, 1946.

Wilson, Robert A. and Bill Hosokawa, *East To America A History of The Japanese In The United States,* Wm. Morrow & Co., New York, 1980.

Winther, Oscar O., *Via Western Express & Stagecoach,* Stanford University Press, Stanford, California, 1945.

Periodicals

California Historical Society, "Stephen Hodge Mann, Stockton Pioneer (his correspondence 1848-1864)," *California Historical Society Quarterly,* Volume 31, Number 3, San Francisco, September, 1952.

Carter, John D., "George Kenyon Fitch, Pioneer California Journalist," *California Historical Society Quarterly,* Volume 20, San Francisco, 1941.

Dun, Marie D., "January 8, 1864, Letter From Hannah Lloyd Neall," *California Historical Society Quarterly,* Volume 31, Number 3, San Francisco, September, 1952.

Ehrman, Sidney M., "Timothy Hopkins, 1859-1936," *California Historical Society Quarterly,* Volume 15, San Francisco, 1936.

Fairchild, M. D., "Reminiscences of A Forty-Niner," *California Historical Society Quarterly,* Volume 13, Number 1, San Francisco, March, 1934.

Vassault, F., "A Story In Transition," *The Overland Monthly,* January, 1891.

Vischer, Eduard, "Californischer Staats-Kalender" (A Trip To The Mining Regions In The Spring of 1859), *California Historical Society Quarterly,* Volume 2, San Francisco, 1932.

Viviano, Frank, "The Asianization of California (and vice versa)," *Golden State Report,* Sacramento, California, August, 1986.

Wheat, Carl I., Editor, "California's Bantam Cock, The Journals of Charles E. DeLong, 1854-1863," *California Historical Society Quarterly,* Volume 9, San Francisco, 1930.

Watkins, T. H., "Who Killed The Railroad Hotel In Auburn?", *Westways,* April, 1971, Volume 63, Part 1.

Wooster, Clarence M., "Railroading In California In The Seventies," *California Historical Society Quarterly,* Volume 18, San Francisco, 1939.

Newspapers

Auburn Journal
Auburn Journal & Placer County Republican
Placer County Republican
Placer Weekly Argus
Sacramento Bee
Sacramento Union
The Journal Republican
The Placer Herald

Miscellaneous

Army Service Forces Annual Reports for Calender Years 1944 and 1945, Auburn-Placer County Library, Auburn, California.
Auburn City, Placer County, Census, Auburn-Placer County Library, Auburn, California.
Auburn City Directory, 1899-1900, compiled and published by J. A. Predom and T. H. Rush.
Burns, Irene A., unpublished writings, Archives, Placer County Office of Education, Auburn, California.
Delmar, Josephine Filcher and Frank Delmar, private documents concerning the Honorable J. A. Filcher and the Adams "Acorn" Press.
Judgment Books, Placer County Recorder's Office, Auburn, California.
Minute Books, Teachers Institute, Archives, Placer County Office of Education, Auburn, California.
Placer Weekly Argus, *Placer County Business & Official Directory, 1875,* Auburn, California, 1875.
Wood, Dallas E., Editor, *History of Palo Alto,* 1939.

Illustration Credits

California State Archives
Office of the Secretary of State
1020 O Street, Room 130
Sacramento, CA 95814
page 27

California State Railroad Museum Library
113 I Street
Sacramento, CA 95814
page 89

Northern Map Company
Dunnellon, Florida 32630
pages 15, 16, 36, 47, 58, 75 and 82

Department of Parks and Recreation
State Historical Resources Commission
830 S Street
Sacramento, CA 95811
pages 23 and 116

The Huntington
1151 Oxford Road
San Marino, CA 91108
page 48

United States Department of the Interior
Geological Survey
345 Middlefield Road
Menlo Park, CA 94025
page 60

The Bancroft Library
Pictorial Collection
University of California
Berkeley, CA 94720
page 24

Pete Hawkins
Auburn, CA
page 93 (upper)

Porret's Type Catalog
page 10 (cut)

Lee Photography
819 Lincoln Way
Auburn, CA 95603
pages 51, 52, 59, 66, 69, 71, 73, 74, 78, 79, 86, 91, 92, 94, 96, 97, 105, 106, 107, 114 and 117

California State Library
Library-Courts Building
P. O. Box 2037
Sacramento, CA 95809
pages 14, 18, 28(left), 39, 44, 49, 56, 57, 70, 80, 98 and 119

Auburn-Placer County Museum
350 Nevada Street
Auburn, CA 95603
pages 22, 63, 81(cut), 83 and 88

Placer County Museum
1273 High Street
Auburn, CA 95603
pages 3, 29, 32, 34, 40, 90 and 101

Placer County Clerk-Recorder
175 Fulweiler Street
Auburn, CA 95603
pages 54, 64, 76(insert) and 87(upper)

Illustrations and Photos by MEG
P. O. Box 597
Newcastle, CA 95658
Cover, Title Page, Map(facing page 1), pages 7, 10(drawing), 21, 28(right), 37, 50, 65, 81(graphics), 85, 93(lower), 99, 104, 109, 111, 121 and 113(lower)

Gilberg Collection
P. O. Box 597
Newcastle, CA 95658
pages 6, 8, 12, 87(lower) and 113(upper)

COLOPHON

This book has been designed by M.E. Gilberg.

Typesetting is by R.L. Gilberg using Aldine Roman typeface.

Printing and binding is by Spilman Printing Co., Sacramento, CA